Science made easy

Key Stage 2 upper
Ages 9-11 Workbook 2

Materials and Their Properties

Authors
Mike Evans and Linda Ellis

Consultant
David Evans

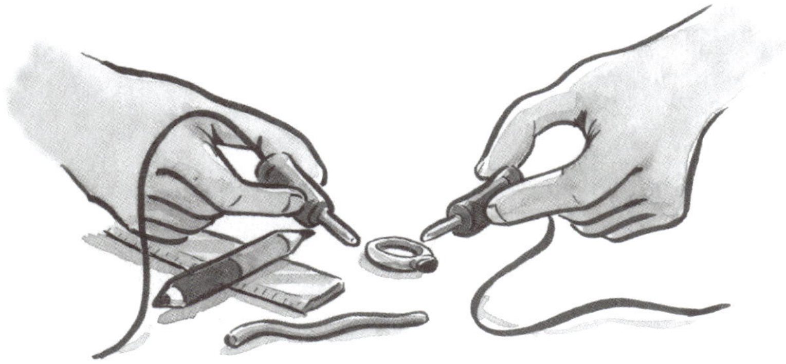

DK

LONDON • NEW YORK • MUNICH • MELBOURNE • DELHI

Which metal is this?

Science facts

A metal is a type of material. Almost all metals are shiny, malleable (can be hammered into different shapes) and conduct heat and electricity. There are different types of metals, such as iron, copper, gold, lead and tin. Each metal has a set of additional properties that makes it unique.

Science quiz

Use the branching key below to identify each of the five metals in this chart. Write the correct letter for each metal below its name.

Metal	Properties
A	hard; brown in colour; good conductor of electricity
B	relatively soft; yellow colour; does not tarnish; very good conductor of electricity
C	soft; silver colour; tarnishes quickly; very heavy; a weak conductor of electricity
D	hard; silver colour; magnetic; tarnishes easily (rusts)
E	hard; silver colour; does not tarnish easily; not magnetic

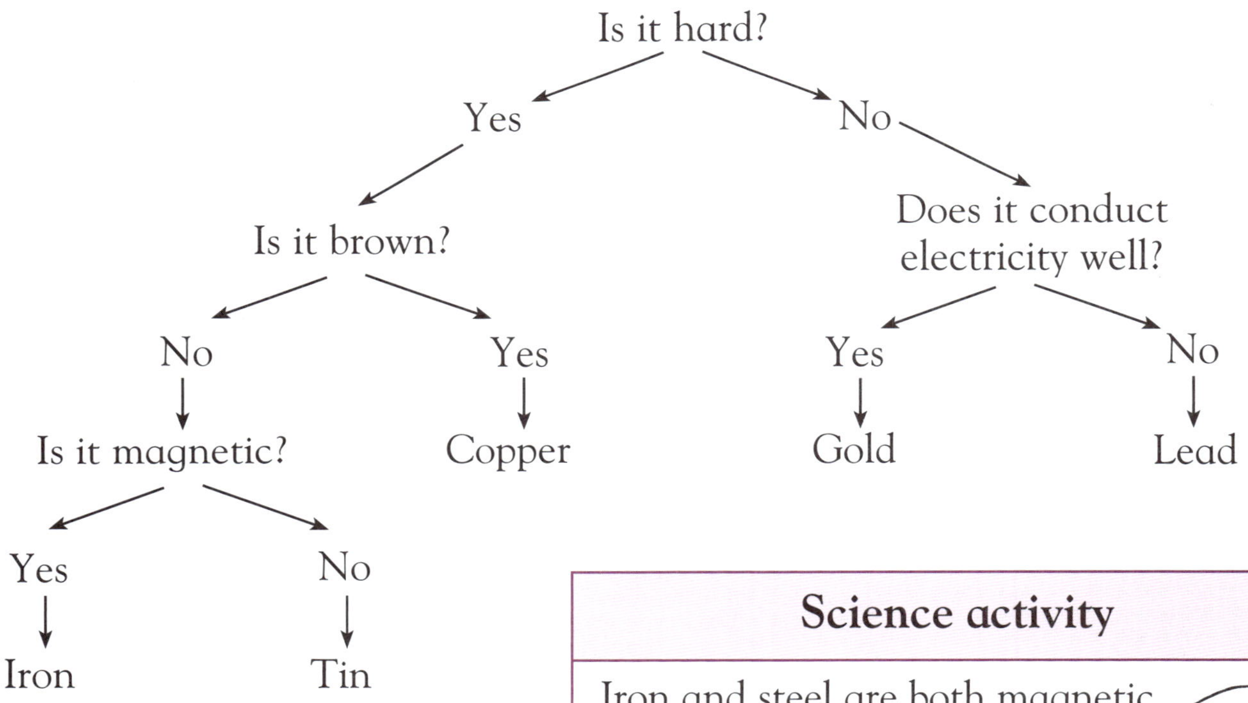

Science activity

Iron and steel are both magnetic. Use a magnet to find out which objects in your home are made of iron or steel.

Which fabric will stretch the most?

Science facts

Materials that stretch easily are called elastic materials. Some materials are more elastic than others. We can compare the elasticity of two materials by hanging equal weights from them and measuring how much they stretch.

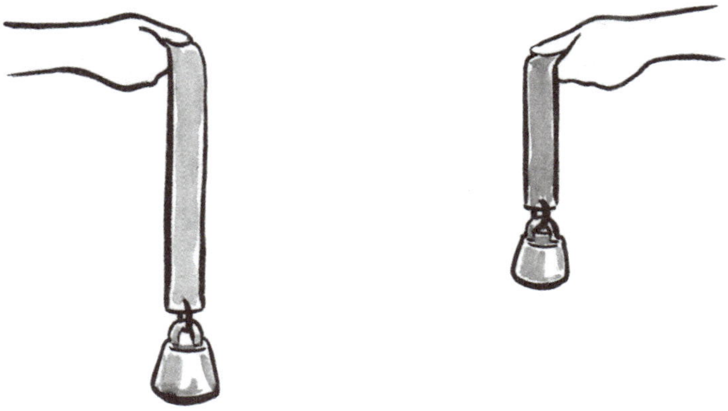

Science quiz

Susan tried to compare the stretch in five different fabrics. All the fabrics were the same length to begin with. Her table of results is shown below.

Fabric	Weight hung from fabric	Amount of stretch
Cotton	10 N	3 cm
Wool	100 N	40 cm
Nylon	100 N	55 cm
Polyester	500 N	200 cm
Tercel	10 N	3 cm

Which material stretched the most?

....

How could Susan have improved her experiment?

....

....

Science activity

Design an experiment to find out which brand of tights stretches the most.

Is it an electrical conductor?

Science facts

A material that allows electricity to pass through it easily is called an electrical conductor. Many metals are good electrical conductors.

Science quiz

An electrical circuit was set up to test whether or not some materials are conductors. If the material conducts electricity, the bulb in the circuit lights up. The better the conductor, the brighter the bulb. Here are the results.

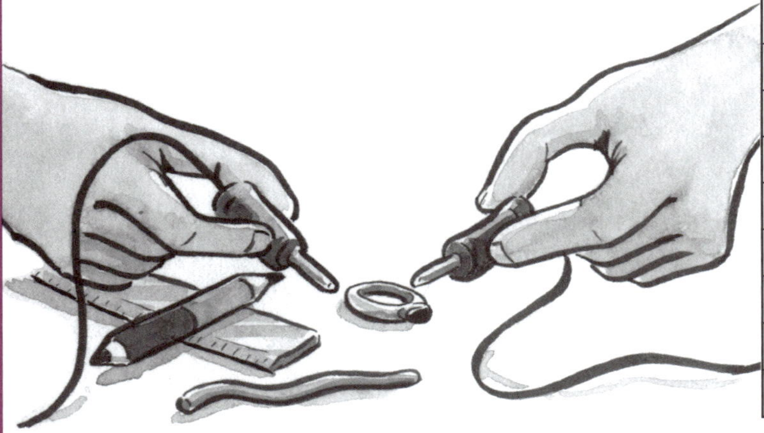

Material tested	Status of lamp
gold	very bright
copper	bright
plastic	not lit
wood	not lit
graphite	quite bright
lead	quite bright
paper	not lit
sea water	bright
pure water	not lit

Most metals conduct electricity. Can you identify the metals in the chart?

Which one is the best conductor?

Which solid non-metal conducts electricity? Where do you usually find this?

Why do you think sea water conducts electricity but pure water does not?

(!) Make a circuit using a battery, wires and a bulb. Use your circuit to find some more materials that conduct electricity.

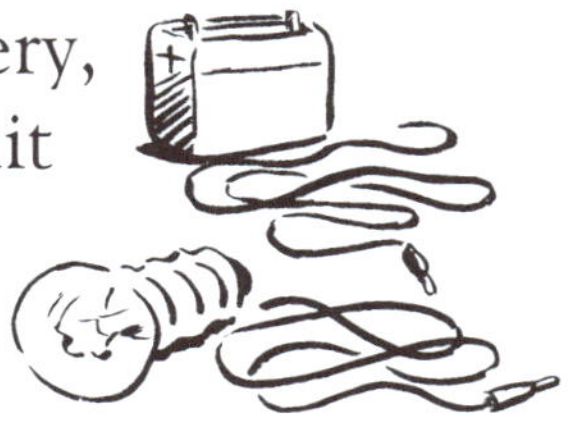

Is it a thermal insulator?

Science facts

Materials that allow heat to pass through them easily are called thermal conductors. Metals and glass are good thermal conductors. Some materials do not conduct heat well. They are called thermal insulators. Materials such as plastics, wood, wool and air are good thermal insulators.

Science quiz

Five glasses containing water at 60°C were each wrapped in a different material. After 10 minutes, the water temperature in each glass was recorded. The results are shown in the table below.

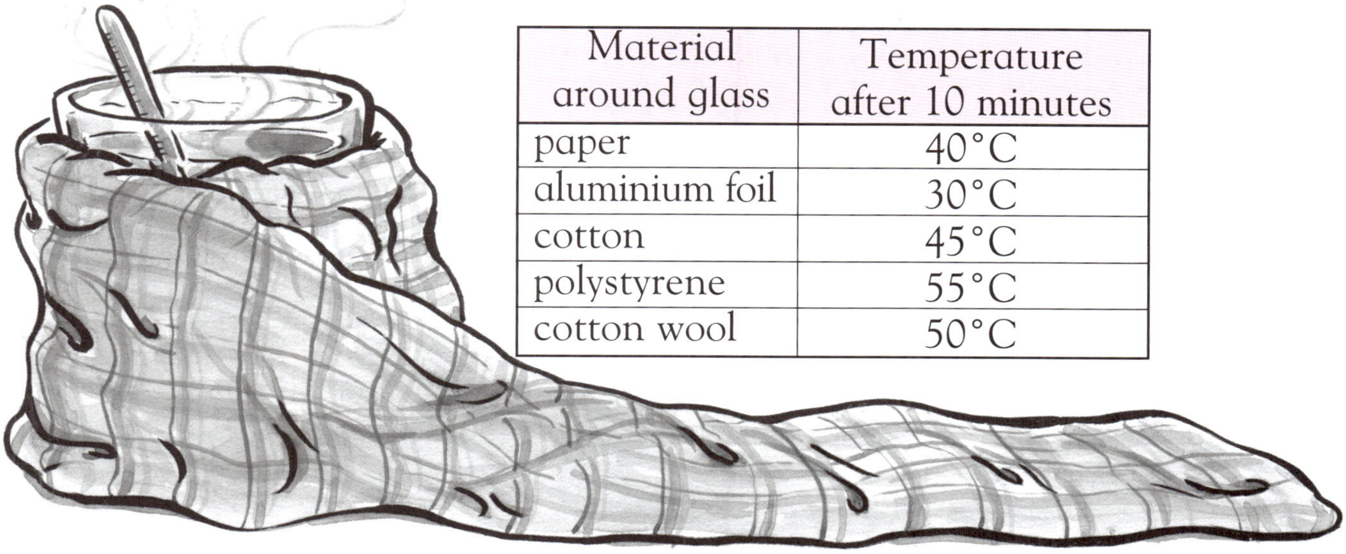

Material around glass	Temperature after 10 minutes
paper	40°C
aluminium foil	30°C
cotton	45°C
polystyrene	55°C
cotton wool	50°C

Which material would you choose to wrap around a water pipe in winter to stop the water from freezing? Explain why.

....

....

....

Science activity

Fill two yoghurt pots with water. Record the temperature in each pot, then put on the lids. Cover one pot in a thick layer of lard. Put them both in a freezer for 20 minutes, then record the water temperature again. What do your results tell you about why whales and seals living in cold waters have thick layers of body fat?

Which is the strongest wood?

Science facts

Strength is an important property of materials. It is a measure of a material's resistance to breaking. You can compare the strengths of different materials by hanging increasingly heavier weights from them until they break.

Science quiz

Lata hung weights on strips of wood until the wood broke in the middle.

Type of wood	Weight needed to break wood (in newtons)
beech	2000 N
oak	3000 N
walnut	2600 N
ash	2500 N
pine	500 N
sycamore	2500 N

Use the data in the table above to work out which type of wood you would choose to build a bridge. Explain your choice.

Science activity

(!) Collect some twigs of the same width from different types of trees. Hang a bag from each twig, then suspend the twigs between two table tops. Load each bag with the same weight (such as a can of beans) until the twigs break. Which is the strongest twig?

Is it a solid, a liquid or a gas?

Science facts

Materials can be grouped as solids, liquids or gases. Solids are substances that retain their shape and do not flow. Liquids flow and take the shape of the container they are in. Gases also flow and fill all the space available.

Science quiz

Which of these materials are solids, which are gases and which are liquids? Write **S**, **G**, or **L** in each box.

Cotton

Plastic

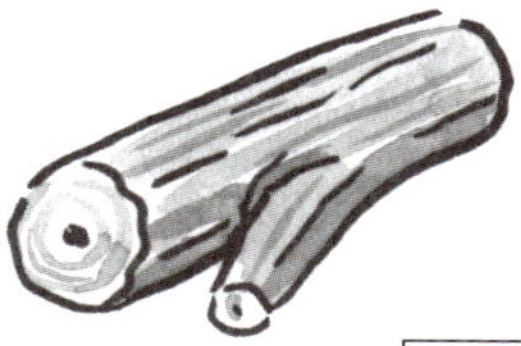
Wood

Jelly

Air

Water vapour

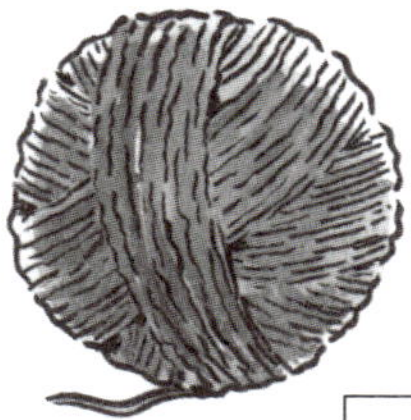
Wool

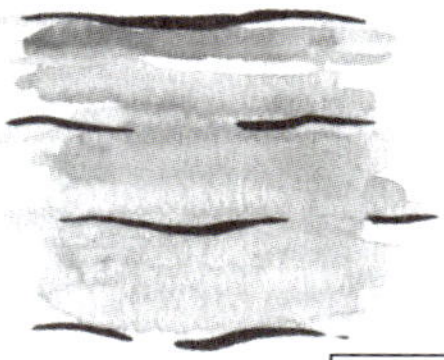
Water

Milk

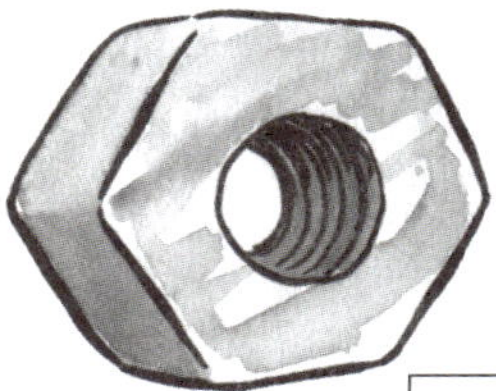
Metal

Silk

Oxygen

Science activity

Find an old bicycle pump. Fill the pump with air, place your finger over the hole, and push down the pump handle. What do you feel? Fill the pump with water, place your finger over the hole, and push the pump handle. What do you feel? Fill the pump with sand, place your finger over the hole, and push the pump handle. What do you feel?

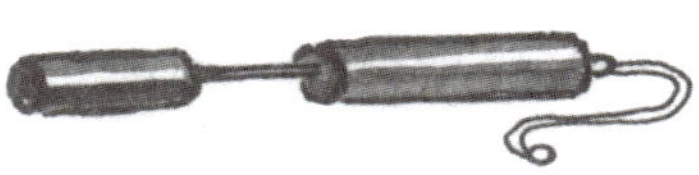

Which is the hardest material?

Science facts

Hardness is the ability of a material to resist scratching. The scientist Friedrich Mohs invented a scale of hardness based on the ability of one natural material to scratch another. Talc is the softest: it can be scratched by all other materials. Gypsum is harder: it can scratch talc but not calcite, which is even harder.

Science quiz

Mohs' scale of hardness is given below. It shows the hardness of different materials on a scale of 1 to 10.

Mohs' scale of hardness		
1	talc	softest
2	gypsum	
3	calcite	
4	fluorite	
5	apatite	
6	orthoclase	
7	quartz	
8	topaz	
9	corundum	
10	diamond	hardest

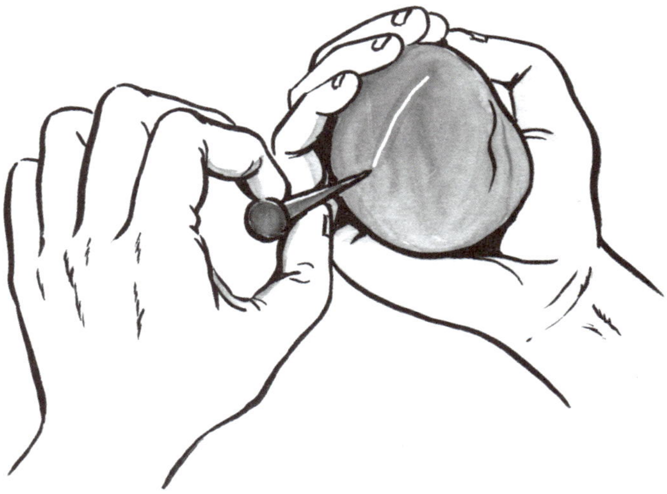

Use the table above to work out approximately how the following materials would rate on Mohs' scale of hardness.

A finger nail – it can scratch gypsum but not calcite. ....

An iron nail – it can scratch apatite but not orthoclase. ....

Glass – it can scratch fluorite. ....

Science activity

(!) Another way to compare the hardness of materials is by doing a simple scratch test using an iron nail. Collect different materials, including stone, wood and metal. Use a nail to test them, then list them in order of hardness. Are any of the materials harder than the iron nail?

Which gas flows the quickest?

Science facts

Gases flow and spread out filling all the available space. Different gases flow at different rates. Some spread very quickly because they are light. Others, such as carbon dioxide, spread more slowly because they are heavy. The scent in perfume is a gas. You can smell it throughout a room.

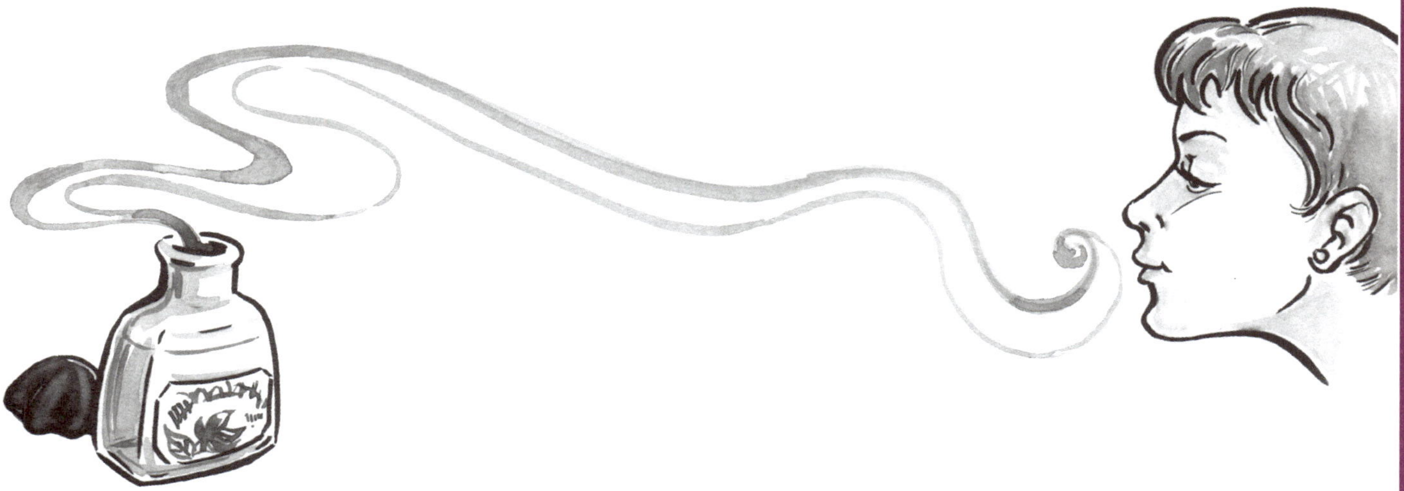

Science quiz

If you were given two different perfumes, how would you work out which scent flowed more quickly?

How would you make your test fair?

Science activity

(!) Carbon dioxide is quite a heavy gas. Carbon dioxide is the "fizz" in fizzy drinks. It is also used in fire extinguishers. Try placing a balloon over the mouth of a large bottle of lemonade or cola. Gently shake the bottle until you partially inflate the balloon. Now take this balloon, and gently release the gas above a lighted candle. What happens? What does this tell you about carbon dioxide? (Do not light the candle without permission from an adult. Make sure there is nothing near the candle that could catch fire.)

Which gas is it?

Science facts

Air is a mixture of gases. The main gases in air are nitrogen and oxygen. There are also small amounts of other gases, including carbon dioxide, helium and argon. Each of these gases has different properties that are useful to us in different ways. They can be separated from each other by cooling because each one condenses at a different temperature.

Science quiz

The properties of some of the gases in air are listed below. A chemically reactive gas can react with other substances to form new substances. Oxygen is chemically reactive; it causes iron to rust.

Gas	Properties
oxygen	chemically reactive; necessary for burning, and for living things to respire (use food for energy)
carbon dioxide	chemically reactive; extinguishes flames; quite a dense (heavy) gas; needed by plants for photosynthesis
argon	not chemically reactive

Decide which gas should be used in each of the following cases.

Filling cylinders to help people with lung disease breathe more easily

....

Filling fire extinguishers

....

Filling light bulbs so that the filament does not react chemically

....

Helium is a gas used to fill fairground balloons. What happens when you let go of one of these balloons? What does this tell you about helium?

....

Science activity

Collect a balloon filled with helium, a balloon partially filled with carbon dioxide (see page 9) and a balloon filled with air. Hold them all at arm's length, and let go. What happens? What does this tell you about the properties of each gas?

Do all liquids flow equally well?

Science facts

Liquids flow and take the shape of the container into which they are poured. Some liquids feel "thin" and flow quickly, while others feel "thick" and flow slowly. This property of resistance to flow is called viscosity.

Science quiz

Jim tested the viscosity of different liquids by pouring each one into a tall jar and timing how long it took for a small lump of modelling clay to drop to the bottom.

Look at the chart below, then number the liquids in order of their viscosity. Write **1** for the least viscous liquid and **7** for the most viscous.

Liquid	Time taken (for modelling clay to fall)	Order
water	2 seconds	
vegetable oil	4.5 seconds	
olive oil	6 seconds	
nail-polish remover	1 second	
golden syrup	90 seconds	
motor oil	10 seconds	
dish-washing liquid	7 seconds	

How long do you think the modelling clay would take to fall through apple juice. Why?

....

....

Science activity

(!) You can compare the viscosity of liquids by comparing how easy they are to pour. Collect different liquids, and try the experiment for yourself. List the liquids in order of their viscosity.

Do rocks absorb water?

Science facts

Different types of rocks are formed in different ways. Each type of rock has a different set of properties. One property of a rock is its porosity. This is the ability of the rock to absorb water. Water is held in rocks under the ground. The more porous the rock, the more water it can hold.

Science quiz

Some rocks were weighed. They were placed in water for an hour and then weighed again.

Rock	Weight before	Weight after
granite	100 N	101 N
chalk	50 N	100 N
sandstone	100 N	150 N
marble	75 N	76 N

Which rock absorbed the most water for its weight?

....

What sorts of plants do you think will grow in areas where granite is the underlying rock? Use the chart above to help you answer this question.

....

....

Science activity

You can check the porosity of materials in a different way. Collect two different bricks. Place each one in a bowl of shallow water, and leave them for 30 minutes. Take them out, and compare them by looking at how far the water has crept up each brick. Is one brick more porous than the other?

Which rock is this?

Science facts

There are many different types of rock. Some common rocks are granite, chalk, sandstone, limestone, flint and slate. They differ in the way they look and in their properties. Scientists often use keys to help identify rocks.

Science quiz

Use the key below to identify these two rocks.

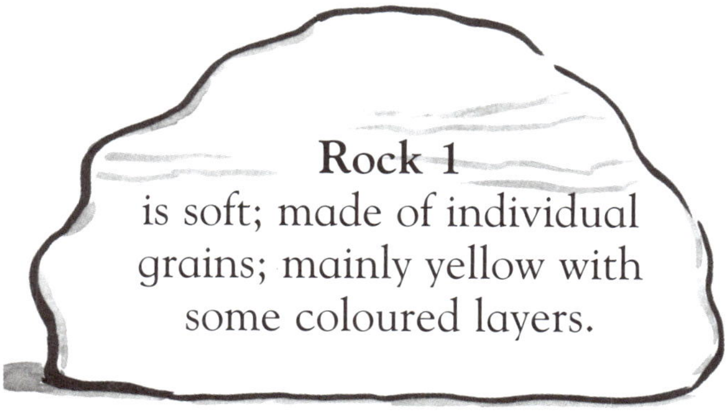

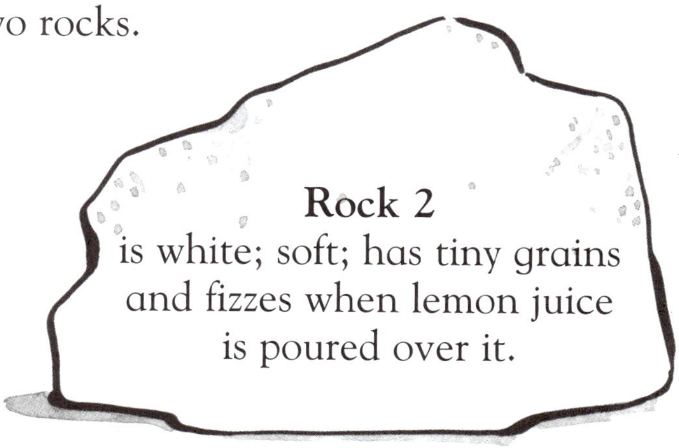

....

Key to some common rocks
1 Does the rock fizz when lemon juice is poured over it? If yes, go to 2; if no, go to 4.
2 Is the rock hard? If yes, it is limestone; if no, then go to 3.
3 The rock is chalk.
4 Does the rock have layers? If yes, go to 7; if no, go to 5.
5 Does the rock contain crystals? If yes, it is granite; if no, go to 6.
6 The rock is flint.
7 Is the rock soft and made of individual grains? If yes, it is sandstone; if no, go to 8.
8 The rock is slate.

Science activity

Keys help to identify things. Different keys help scientists identify different things, such as types of grasses, insects or wild flowers. How good are you at making keys? Collect some objects from home, and make up a key to identify them. Try out your key on someone else. Does it work?

What kind of soil is this?

Science facts

Soil is made up of grains of broken rock and humus (mainly rotted plant material). A soil's type depends on the mix of humus and on the size of the grains of rock. The grains can be very small and smooth, such as in clay, or they can be larger, like grains of sand or even as large as pieces of gravel.

Science quiz

Use this key to identify the soil described below.

The soil is light in colour, gritty and drains well. The soil is ....

Does the soil feel gritty?

- Yes → Is the soil light in colour, and does it drain very quickly?
  - Yes → sandy
  - No → loam
- No → Does the soil have very small grains, and does it hold water?
  - Yes → clay
  - No → peat

Different plants prefer different types of soil. If a plant had roots that could rot very easily in water, which type of soil might help it to grow well?

....

....

Science activity

(!) You can see the different parts that make up a soil by using water to separate them. Pour water into an empty jar until it is three-quarters full. Stir in three or four dessertspoons of soil, and mix well. Allow time for the soil to settle so you can see the different parts. Try different soils. What do they look like?

Which soil is the most permeable?

Science facts

The amount of time water takes to drain through a soil is known as the soil's permeability. Some soils drain easily, others do not. How quickly a soil drains depends on the proportion of humus and on the size of the grains of rock.

Science quiz

Is there a connection between a soil's grain size and how quickly it drains? Make a graph using the data in the table below to answer this question.

Size of grain	Time taken (for 1 litre of water to drain through a cup of soil)
2 mm	60 seconds
1 mm	70 seconds
6 mm	20 seconds
4 mm	40 seconds
3 mm	50 seconds

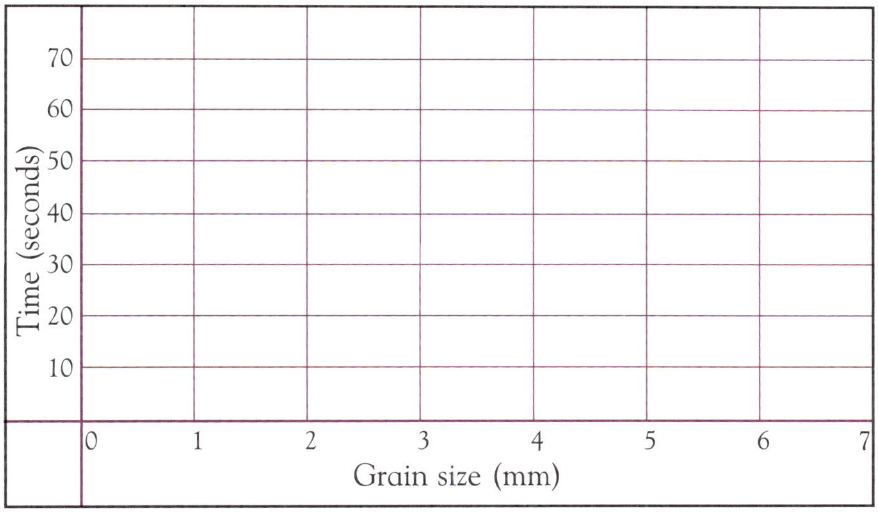

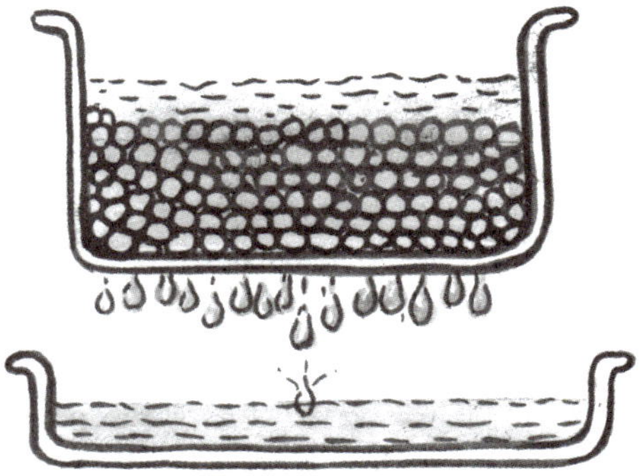

Complete the following sentence.
Water drains more quickly in soils with ....

Science activity

(!) Make a funnel by cutting the top off a plastic bottle. Place a small plug of cotton wool inside the funnel, then fill it with soil. Time how long it takes for a cup of water to drain through. Repeat the experiment using a different soil. Which soil type is likely to have the larger grains? Why?

Which rocks are the most useful?

Science facts

Materials are chosen for use on the basis of their properties. Rocks vary in their properties and are used in a variety of ways, such as in the making of buildings, bridges, statues, roofs, monuments, gravestones and ornaments.

Science quiz

This chart lists some rocks and their properties.

Rock	Properties
limestone	fairly dense; relatively easy to cut; can be shaped into blocks; some forms are white in colour
slate	black in colour; not permeable; formed in layers that can be split up easily
granite	dense; can be cut, carved and shaped; is resistant to water and pollution; has a range of colours
marble	dense; good range of colours; can be carved and shaped; strong
malachite	attractive green colours; can be cut and shaped

Draw a line linking each rock listed below to one or more of the uses on the right. Use the properties of the rocks given above to help you.

Rocks	Uses
limestone	roofing material
malachite	statue
granite	pillars to support a bridge
marble	monument designed to last
slate	chess set

Science activity

(!) Collect a lump of chalk and a file. Can you shape the lump to make a stick of drawing chalk? What does this tell you about the properties of chalk?

Answer Section with Parents' Notes

Key Stage 2 upper
Ages 9–11
Materials and Their Properties

This section provides explanatory notes and answers to all the *Science quizzes*. Read through each page together, and ensure that your child understands each task. Point out any mistakes in your child's work, and correct any errors, but also remember to praise your child's efforts and achievements. Where appropriate, ask your child to predict the outcome of the *Science activities*. After each activity, challenge your child to explain his or her results.

When handling soil, make sure that gloves are worn and that hands are washed afterwards.

2

Which metal is this?

Science facts
A metal is a type of material. Almost all metals are shiny, malleable (can be hammered into different shapes) and conduct heat and electricity. There are different types of metals, such as iron, copper, gold, lead and tin. Each metal has a set of additional properties that makes it unique.

Science quiz
Use the branching key below to identify each of the five metals in this chart. Write the correct letter for each metal below its name.

Metal	Properties
A	hard; brown in colour; good conductor of electricity
B	relatively soft; yellow colour; does not tarnish; very good conductor of electricity
C	soft; silver colour; tarnishes quickly; very heavy; a weak conductor of electricity
D	hard; silver colour; magnetic; tarnishes easily (rusts)
E	hard; silver colour; does not tarnish easily; not magnetic

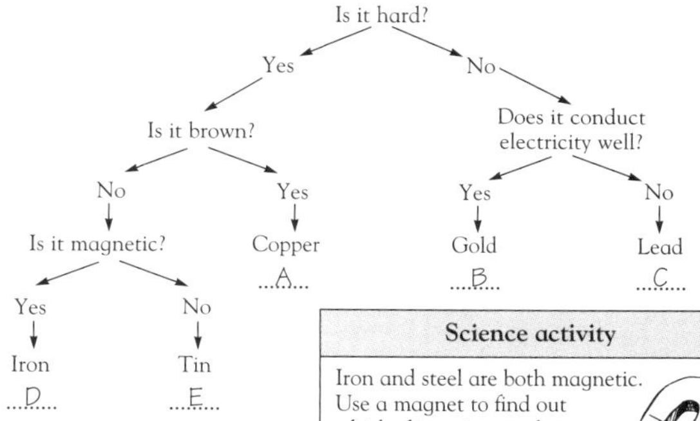

Science activity

Iron and steel are both magnetic. Use a magnet to find out which objects in your home are made of iron or steel.

Your child can use a magnet to check the magnetic properties of objects such as pipes, cutlery, toys, appliances, coins and keys. Note that some stainless steel cutlery may not be magnetic, while some coins made of copper-coated steel are magnetic.

3

Which fabric will stretch the most?

Science facts
Materials that stretch easily are called elastic materials. Some materials are more elastic than others. We can compare the elasticity of two materials by hanging equal weights from them and measuring how much they stretch.

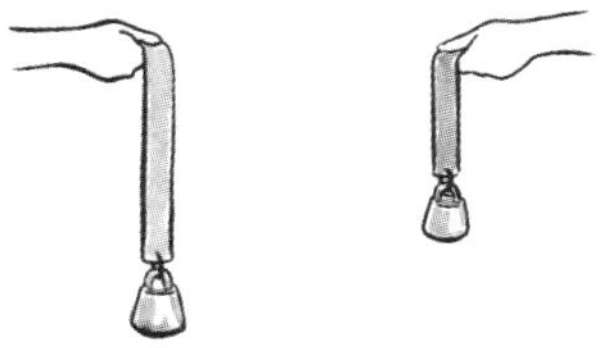

Science quiz
Susan tried to compare the stretch in five different fabrics. All the fabrics were the same length to begin with. Her table of results is shown below.

Fabric	Weight hung from fabric	Amount of stretch
cotton	10 N	3 cm
wool	100 N	40 cm
nylon	100 N	55 cm
polyester	500 N	200 cm
tercel	10 N	3 cm

Which material stretched the most?
Nylon stretched the most. It stretched 5.5 cm for every 10 N.

How could Susan have improved her experiment?
Susan could have improved her experiment by using the same weight each time to allow a comparision to be made more easily.

Science activity

Design an experiment to find out which brand of tights stretches the most.

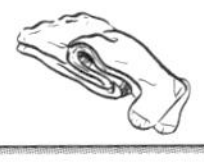

From the table in the quiz, it may seem that polyester stretched the most, but that is because Susan used a greater weight to stretch it. For the activity, encourage your child to design a fair test, using the same weight for each brand of tights.

4

Is it an electrical conductor?

Science facts
A material that allows electricity to pass through it easily is called an electrical conductor. Many metals are good electrical conductors.

Science quiz
An electrical circuit was set up to test whether or not some materials are conductors. If the material conducts electricity, the bulb in the circuit lights up. The better the conductor, the brighter the bulb. Here are the results.

Material tested	Status of lamp
gold	very bright
copper	bright
plastic	not lit
wood	not lit
graphite	quite bright
lead	quite bright
paper	not lit
sea water	bright
pure water	not lit

Most metals conduct electricity. Can you identify the metals in the chart?
Gold, copper and lead.

Which one is the best conductor? Gold is the best conductor.

Which solid non-metal conducts electricity? Where do you usually find this?
Graphite conducts electricity. It is often found in pencils.

Why do you think sea water conducts electricity but pure water does not?
The dissolved salt in sea water makes it conduct electricity.

Science activity

(!) Make a circuit using a battery, wires and a bulb. Use your circuit to find some more materials that conduct electricity.

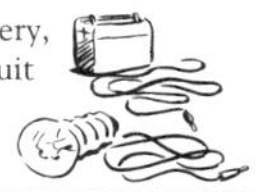

Assist your child in testing the conductivity of different materials. Metals are generally good conductors of electricity. Two non-metallic conductors are: graphite, a form of carbon found in pencil "lead", and sea water, which contains salt.

5 Is it a thermal insulator? ☆

Science facts
Materials that allow heat to pass through them easily are called thermal conductors. Metals and glass are good thermal conductors. Some materials do not conduct heat well. They are called thermal insulators. Materials such as plastics, wood, wool and air are good thermal insulators.

Science quiz
Five glasses containing water at 60°C were each wrapped in a different material. After 10 minutes, the water temperature in each glass was recorded. The results are shown in the table below.

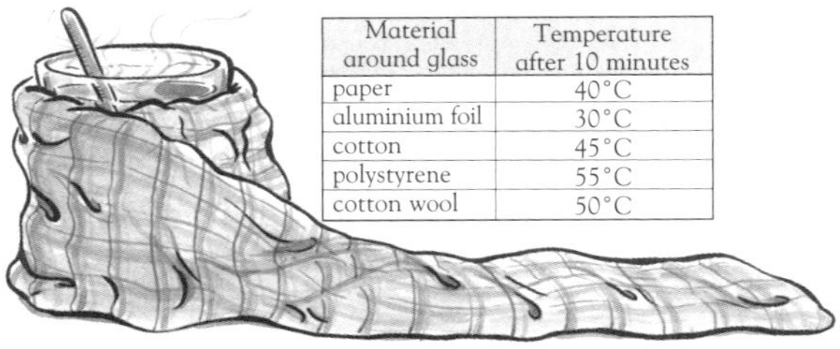

Material around glass	Temperature after 10 minutes
paper	40°C
aluminium foil	30°C
cotton	45°C
polystyrene	55°C
cotton wool	50°C

Which material would you choose to wrap around a water pipe in winter to stop the water from freezing? Explain why.

I would wrap polystyrene around a water pipe to stop the water from freezing because the experiment shows that it is the best thermal insulator – it kept the water warm the longest.

Science activity

Fill two yoghurt pots with water. Record the temperature in each pot, then put on the lids. Cover one pot in a thick layer of lard. Put them both in a freezer for 20 minutes, then record the water temperature again. What do your results tell you about why whales and seals living in cold waters have thick layers of body fat?

The quiz shows that some materials are better thermal insulators than others. For the activity, encourage your child to predict which yoghurt pot will stay warmer and why. He or she will learn that body fat is a good thermal insulator.

6 ☆ Which is the strongest wood?

Science facts
Strength is an important property of materials. It is a measure of a material's resistance to breaking. You can compare the strengths of different materials by hanging increasingly heavier weights from them until they break.

Science quiz
Lata hung weights on strips of wood until the wood broke in the middle.

Type of wood	Weight needed to break wood (in newtons)
beech	2000 N
oak	3000 N
walnut	2600 N
ash	2500 N
pine	500 N
sycamore	2500 N

Use the data in the table above to work out which type of wood you would choose to build a bridge. Explain your choice.

I would choose oak to build a bridge because the experiment shows that it is the strongest wood.

Science activity

(!) Collect some twigs of the same width from different types of trees. Hang a bag from each twig, then suspend the twigs between two table tops. Load each bag with the same weight (such as a can of beans) until the twigs break. Which is the strongest twig?

Your child will learn how to compare the strength of different materials. Oak was the strongest of the woods tested, but was it a fair test? The experiment would only be fair if all the twigs were of the same length and thickness.

7 Is it a solid, a liquid or a gas? ☆

Science facts
Materials can be grouped as solids, liquids or gases. Solids are substances that retain their shape and do not flow. Liquids flow and take the shape of the container they are in. Gases also flow and fill all the space available.

Science quiz
Which of these materials are solids, which are gases and which are liquids? Write **S**, **G**, or **L** in each box.

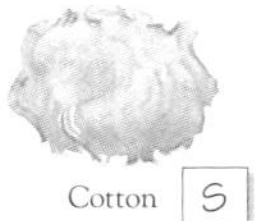
Cotton S

Plastic S

Wood S

Jelly S

Air G

Water vapour G

Wool S

Water L

Milk L

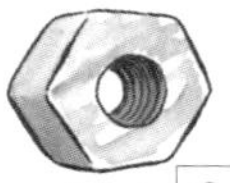
Metal S

Silk S

Oxygen G

Science activity

Find an old bicycle pump. Fill the pump with air, place your finger over the hole, and push down the pump handle. What do you feel? Fill the pump with water, place your finger over the hole, and push the pump handle. What do you feel? Fill the pump with sand, place your finger over the hole, and push the pump handle. What do you feel?

All substances are made of particles (atoms and molecules). These are further apart in a gas than in a solid or a liquid and can be pushed together by compression. Your child will find that you can compress air (a gas) but not liquids and solids.

8 ☆ Which is the hardest material?

Science facts
Hardness is the ability of a material to resist scratching. The scientist Friedrich Mohs invented a scale of hardness based on the ability of one natural material to scratch another. Talc is the softest: it can be scratched by all other materials. Gypsum is harder: it can scratch talc but not calcite, which is even harder.

Science quiz
Mohs' scale of hardness is given below. It shows the hardness of different materials on a scale of 1 to 10.

Mohs' scale of hardness	
1 talc	softest
2 gypsum	
3 calcite	
4 fluorite	
5 apatite	
6 orthoclase	
7 quartz	
8 topaz	
9 corundum	
10 diamond	hardest

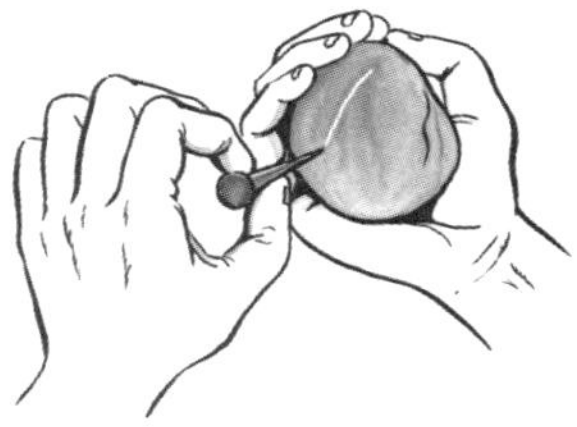

Use the table above to work out approximately how the following materials would rate on Mohs' scale of hardness.

A finger nail – it can scratch gypsum but not calcite. About 2·5

An iron nail – it can scratch apatite but not orthoclase. About 5·5

Glass – it can scratch fluorite. Higher than 4

Science activity

(!) Another way to compare the hardness of materials is by doing a simple scratch test using an iron nail. Collect different materials, including stone, wood and metal. Use a nail to test them, then list them in order of hardness. Are any of the materials harder than the iron nail?

Some materials tested in the activity may not be scratched by the nail. Encourage your child to come up with a way to test these harder materials. Suggest that something harder (such as a diamond) may be needed to scratch them.

9 Which gas flows the quickest?

Science facts

Gases flow and spread out filling all the available space. Different gases flow at different rates. Some spread very quickly because they are light. Others, such as carbon dioxide, spread more slowly because they are heavy. The scent in perfume is a gas. You can smell it throughout a room.

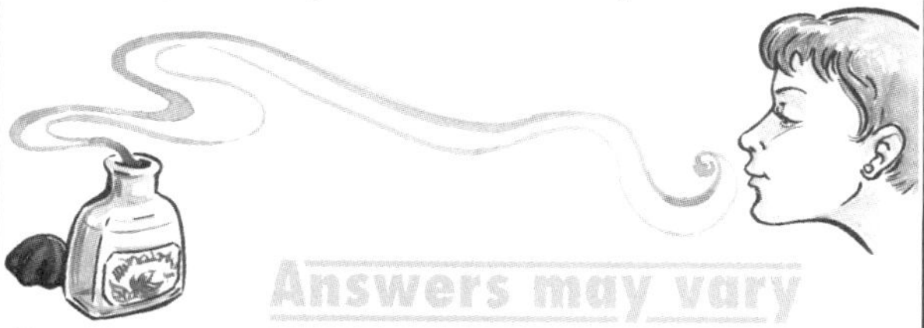

Science quiz

If you were given two different perfumes, how would you work out which scent flowed more quickly?

Place the perfumes at one end of a room and seat a person at the other end to detect which smell arrives first.

How would you make your test fair?

To make the test fair, the bottles must be the same distance away from the tester and the tops removed at the same time.

Science activity

(!) Carbon dioxide is quite a heavy gas. Carbon dioxide is the "fizz" in fizzy drinks. It is also used in fire extinguishers. Try placing a balloon over the mouth of a large bottle of lemonade or cola. Gently shake the bottle until you partially inflate the balloon. Now take this balloon, and gently release the gas above a lighted candle. What happens? What does this tell you about carbon dioxide? (Do not light the candle without permission from an adult. Make sure there is nothing near the candle that could catch fire.)

From the activity, your child will learn that carbon dioxide extinguishes a flame. Carbon dioxide is a heavy gas. It will eventually mix with the air in the room, but initially it will tend to flow downwards onto the candle.

10 Which gas is it?

Science facts

Air is a mixture of gases. The main gases in air are nitrogen and oxygen. There are also small amounts of other gases, including carbon dioxide, helium and argon. Each of these gases has different properties that are useful to us in different ways. They can be separated from each other by cooling because each one condenses at a different temperature.

Science quiz

The properties of some of the gases in air are listed below. A chemically reactive gas can react with other substances to form new substances. Oxygen is chemically reactive; it causes iron to rust.

Gas	Properties
oxygen	chemically reactive; necessary for burning, and for living things to respire (use food for energy)
carbon dioxide	chemically reactive; extinguishes flames; quite a dense (heavy) gas; needed by plants for photosynthesis
argon	not chemically reactive

Decide which gas should be used in each of the following cases.

Filling cylinders to help people with lung disease breathe more easily	Filling fire extinguishers	Filling light bulbs so that the filament does not react chemically
oxygen	carbon dioxide	argon

Helium is a gas used to fill fairground balloons. What happens when you let go of one of these balloons? What does this tell you about helium?

Helium balloons float upwards because helium is lighter than air.

Science activity

Collect a balloon filled with helium, a balloon partially filled with carbon dioxide (see page 9) and a balloon filled with air. Hold them all at arm's length, and let go. What happens? What does this tell you about the properties of each gas?

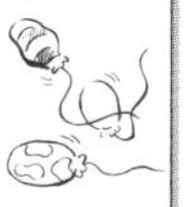

Ask your child to predict what will happen to the balloons before trying the activity. Explain that helium is lighter than air and carbon dioxide is heavier. The helium-filled balloon will rise up while the one with carbon dioxide will come down quickly.

11 Do all liquids flow equally well?

Science facts

Liquids flow and take the shape of the container into which they are poured. Some liquids feel "thin" and flow quickly, while others feel "thick" and flow slowly. This property of resistance to flow is called viscosity.

Science quiz

Jim tested the viscosity of different liquids by pouring each one into a tall jar and timing how long it took for a small lump of modelling clay to drop to the bottom.

Look at the chart below, then number the liquids in order of their viscosity. Write **1** for the least viscous liquid and **7** for the most viscous.

Liquid	Time taken (for modelling clay to fall)	Order
water	2 seconds	2
vegetable oil	4.5 seconds	3
olive oil	6 seconds	4
nail-polish remover	1 second	1
golden syrup	90 seconds	7
motor oil	10 seconds	6
dish-washing liquid	7 seconds	5

How long do you think the modelling clay would take to fall through apple juice? Why?

The modelling clay would probably take just over 2 seconds to fall through apple juice because apple juice is mostly water.

Science activity

(!) You can compare the viscosity of liquids by comparing how easy they are to pour. Collect different liquids, and try the experiment for yourself. List the liquids in order of their viscosity.

Make sure none of the liquids your child uses for pouring are hazardous. Discuss the relative merits of the experiment in the quiz and in the activity. The pouring experiment is quick and easy but not as accurate as the one using modelling clay.

12 Do rocks absorb water?

Science facts

Different types of rocks are formed in different ways. Each type of rock has a different set of properties. One property of a rock is its porosity. This is the ability of the rock to absorb water. Water is held in rocks under the ground. The more porous the rock, the more water it can hold.

Science quiz

Some rocks were weighed. They were placed in water for an hour and then weighed again.

Rock	Weight before	Weight after
granite	100 N	101 N
chalk	50 N	100 N
sandstone	100 N	150 N
marble	75 N	76 N

Which rock absorbed the most water for its weight?

Chalk absorbed the most water for its weight. Its weight doubled.

What sorts of plants do you think will grow in areas where granite is the underlying rock? Use the chart above to help you answer this question.

Only plants that can survive in dry conditions grow in areas where granite is the underlying rock, as granite does not retain moisture.

Science activity

You can check the porosity of materials in a different way. Collect two different bricks. Place each one in a bowl of shallow water, and leave them for 30 minutes. Take them out, and compare them by looking at how far the water has crept up each brick. Is one brick more porous than the other?

Most bricks absorb moisture. You could take this opportunity to discuss why we need to damp-proof brick buildings. If your home is made of brick, encourage your child to find out what material has been used to guard against dampness.

13 Which rock is this?

Science facts
There are many different types of rock. Some common rocks are granite, chalk, sandstone, limestone, flint and slate. They differ in the way they look and in their properties. Scientists often use keys to help identify rocks.

Science quiz
Use the key below to identify these two rocks.

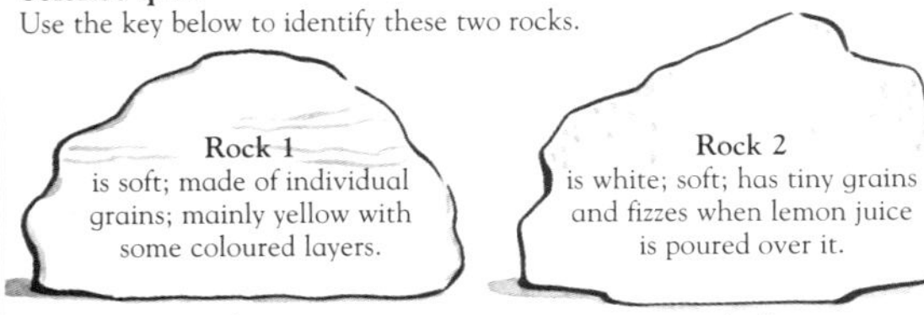

sandstone .... chalk

Key to some common rocks
1 Does the rock fizz when lemon juice is poured over it? If yes, go to 2; if no, go to 4.
2 Is the rock hard? If yes, it is limestone; if no, then go to 3.
3 The rock is chalk.
4 Does the rock have layers? If yes, go to 7; if no, go to 5.
5 Does the rock contain crystals? If yes, it is granite; if no, go to 6.
6 The rock is flint.
7 Is the rock soft and made of individual grains? If yes, it is sandstone; if no, go to 8.
8 The rock is slate.

Science activity

Keys help to identify things. Different keys help scientists identify different things, such as types of grasses, insects or wild flowers. How good are you at making keys? Collect some objects from home, and make up a key to identify them. Try out your key on someone else. Does it work?

Help your child to construct a key by asking questions that can divide things first into two sets, and then divide these sets into subsets, and so on. Encourage your child to try out his or her key and to see if others can make it work.

14 What kind of soil is this?

Science facts
Soil is made up of grains of broken rock and humus (mainly rotted plant material). A soil's type depends on the mix of humus and on the size of the grains of rock. The grains can be very small and smooth, such as in clay, or they can be larger, like grains of sand or even as large as pieces of gravel.

Science quiz
Use this key to identify the soil described below.

The soil is light in colour, gritty and drains well. The soil is ....sandy.........

Does the soil feel gritty?

- Yes → Is the soil light in colour, and does it drain very quickly?
  - Yes → sandy
  - No → loam
- No → Does the soil have very small grains, and does it hold water?
  - Yes → clay
  - No → peat

Different plants prefer different types of soil. If a plant had roots that could rot very easily in water, which type of soil might help it to grow well?
Sandy soil would drain water away from the roots and prevent them from rotting.

Science activity

(!) You can see the different parts that make up a soil by using water to separate them. Pour water into an empty jar until it is three-quarters full. Stir in three or four dessertspoons of soil, and mix well. Allow time for the soil to settle so you can see the different parts. Try different soils. What do they look like?

After mixing water with soil, your child will see layers forming: the humus will float, the heavier grains will sink and the smaller clay particles will form an upper layer. The amount of each component will determine the type of soil.

15 Which soil is the most permeable?

Science facts
The amount of time water takes to drain through a soil is known as the soil's permeability. Some soils drain easily, others do not. How quickly a soil drains depends on the proportion of humus and on the size of the grains of rock.

Science quiz
Is there a connection between a soil's grain size and how quickly it drains? Make a graph using the data in the table below to answer this question.

Size of grain	Time taken (for 1 litre of water to drain through a cup of soil)
2 mm	60 seconds
1 mm	70 seconds
6 mm	20 seconds
4 mm	40 seconds
3 mm	50 seconds

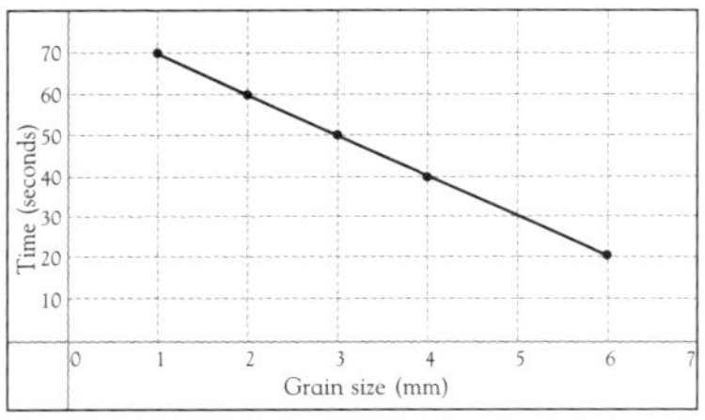

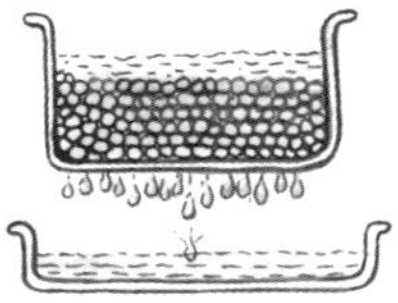

Complete the following sentence.
Water drains more quickly in soils with ....larger grains.........

Science activity

(!) Make a funnel by cutting the top off a plastic bottle. Place a small plug of cotton wool inside the funnel, then fill it with soil. Time how long it takes for a cup of water to drain through. Repeat the experiment using a different soil. Which soil type is likely to have the larger grains? Why?

Ask your child to predict the outcome of the test in the activity. To be fair, your child will need to use the same amount of water and soil each time. As the graph shows in the quiz, water will flow through quicker in soils with larger grains.

16 Which rocks are the most useful?

Science facts
Materials are chosen for use on the basis of their properties. Rocks vary in their properties and are used in a variety of ways, such as in the making of buildings, bridges, statues, roofs, monuments, gravestones and ornaments.

Science quiz Answers may vary
This chart lists some rocks and their properties.

Rock	Properties
limestone	fairly dense; relatively easy to cut; can be shaped into blocks; some forms are white in colour
slate	black in colour; not permeable; formed in layers that can be split up easily
granite	dense; can be cut, carved and shaped; is resistant to water and pollution; has a range of colours
marble	dense; good range of colours; can be carved and shaped; strong
malachite	attractive green colours; can be cut and shaped

Draw a line linking each rock listed below to one or more of the uses on the right. Use the properties of the rocks given above to help you.

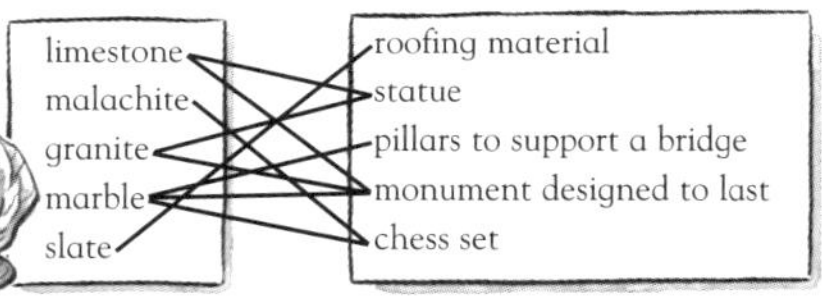

Science activity

(!) Collect a lump of chalk and a file. Can you shape the lump to make a stick of drawing chalk? What does this tell you about the properties of chalk?

The properties of a material will determine how it is used. Chalk can be found quite easily, either in chalk downs or in mineral shops. Encourage your child to feel the chalk. It is very soft compared with other rocks and can be shaped easily.

17 How fast do things cool down?

Science facts
Hot water cools down until it reaches room temperature. There is a pattern in the way things cool down.

Science quiz
Look at the axes on the graph below. Guess the shape of a line showing how hot water cools down. Draw this line on the graph. Julia did an experiment to see what really happens. Her results are shown in the table on the right. Plot her results on your graph. Does it match the drawing you made earlier?

Answers may vary

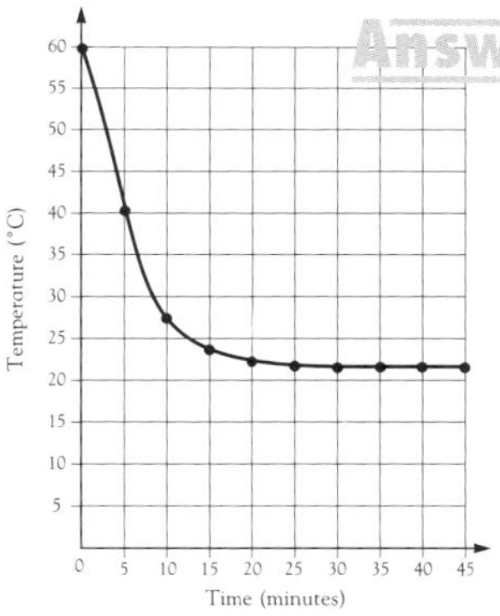

Cooling time	Temperature of water
0 minutes	60°C
5 minutes	40°C
10 minutes	28°C
15 minutes	24°C
20 minutes	23°C
25 minutes	22°C
30 minutes	22°C
35 minutes	22°C

What will the temperature be after 45 minutes? 22°C – room temperature

Science activity

(!) Measure the temperature of some hot water as it cools down. Take the temperature every 3 minutes. Plot a graph of your results. What shape is your graph? Is your graph similar to the one you plotted above?

Your child will notice that the temperature of the hot water falls until it reaches room temperature. It then remains constant. Ask your child to try stirring the water before taking the temperature. Does it make a difference?

18 How quickly does it evaporate?

Science facts
Water left in a bowl will slowly disappear. It turns into water vapour, and mixes with the air. This means the water has evaporated: the liquid has changed into a gas. Some liquids evaporate more quickly than others. Liquids with high boiling points (those that boil at very high temperatures) tend to evaporate more slowly than those with lower boiling points.

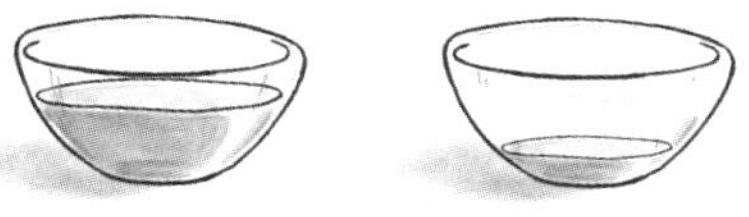

Science quiz
Number the three liquids listed below in order of how fast you would expect them to evaporate. Explain why you think so.

2 nail-polish remover 3 water 1 butane propellant from an aerosol spray

Butane is a gas at room temperature – it has the lowest boiling point. Nail-polish remover has the next lowest boiling point – it evaporates quickly when the lid is removed.

How do you think you could make the water evaporate more quickly?
The water could be made to evaporate more quickly by heating it.

Science activity

Drops of water on your skin evaporate quickly because of the warmth of your body. As the water evaporates, it takes heat from your skin. Smear a few drops of water over the palm of one hand. Do they disappear? Does your palm feel hot or cold?

When liquids are heated, they evaporate, but at different rates depending on their boiling points. The warmth of your child's hand speeds up the water's evaporation. The hand feels cold because as the water evaporates, it takes heat from the hand.

19 Can you separate salt from sand?

Science facts
Filtering removes insoluble particles from water. Salt is soluble in water but sand is not soluble. The water in a salt solution will evaporate if it is left out in the open. Rock salt is a mixture of salt and sand.

Science quiz
Using the information above, explain how you could separate the salt from a piece of rock salt. Drawing a flow chart might help.

Stir the rock salt in water.
↓
Heat the mixture to dissolve all the salt.
↓
Pour the mixture through a filter to remove the sand.
↓
Leave the salt solution to evaporate. You will be left with the salt.

Science activity

What type of paper makes the best filter? Design an experiment to find out. You will need a funnel and different kinds of paper – newspaper, writing paper, blotting paper, wrapping paper and tissue paper.

Help your child to design the experiment for the activity. Ask questions such as, "What shall we filter?", "What should we look at to find out which paper filters best?", "How about looking at how clear the water is after filtration?"

20 Are some changes reversible?

Science facts
When ice is warmed, it melts to form water. When water is heated further, it boils to form water vapour. These changes from solid to liquid to gas can be reversed by cooling water vapour. The water vapour will condense to form water, and the water will freeze to form ice.

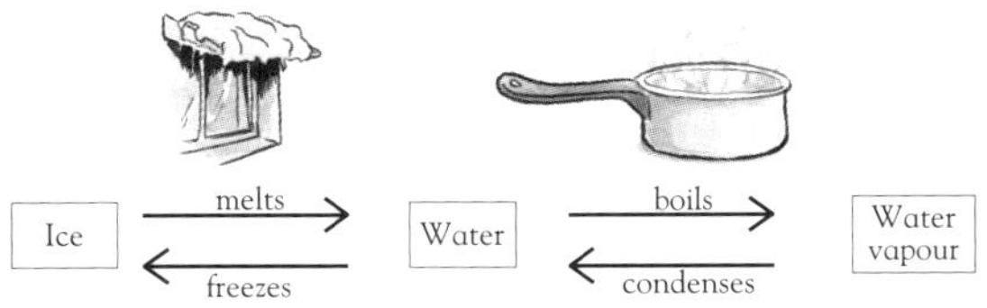

Science quiz
Explain what is happening to the water in each picture.

The water vapour is condensing to form water on the cold window pane.

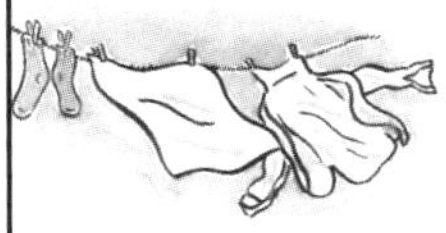

The water in the wet washing is evaporating to form water vapour.

The water vapour in the air is changing to water, then quickly to ice on a very cold day.

Science activity

(!) Light a candle, and watch it carefully (do not touch it or get too close). Can you identify the solid wax, melted wax and wax vapour? Can you see the liquid wax solidifying when the flame is put out?

Candle wax melts to form a liquid. Your child will notice that the candle flame starts a little distance from the wick. This is because the heat from the flame vapourises the molten wax to form invisible wax vapour. It is the wax vapour that burns.

21 Are some changes irreversible?

Science facts
When you mix substances together, they may change to form new substances. The changes can be reversible or irreversible. For instance, when vinegar is mixed with bicarbonate of soda, the two fizz and a new substance is formed. This change is irreversible. A change is likely to be irreversible if there is a reaction, such as a fizz or a temperature change.

Science quiz
Are the following mixing processes reversible or irreversible?

1 Stirring sugar into water .... Reversible

2 Adding water to plaster of Paris .... Irreversible

3 Mixing sand and sugar .... Reversible

4 Adding lemon juice to red cabbage juice (the colour changes from purple to red) .... Reversible

Science activity

Try mixing the following substances.
Which changes are reversible?
1 Lemon juice added to baking powder
2 Vinegar added to chalk
3 Vinegar added to salt
4 Lemon juice added to sugar

Adding an alkali will reverse the colour change in the fourth question in the quiz. Lemon juice and vinegar are acids. They will fizz and produce carbon dioxide when added to carbonates, such as chalk and baking powder.

22 What happens when it burns?

Science facts
Oxygen from the air is needed for something to burn. Burning is an irreversible process that forms new substances. Some of these substances are solids, such as ash or soot, and some are gases, such as water vapour and carbon dioxide. When paper burns, it produces soot, water vapour, carbon dioxide, a small amount of other gases and ash.

Science quiz
Look at the drawing. It shows a candle burning inside an upturned jam jar.

What do you think is produced when the wax burns? Explain why you think this.

The water droplets show that water vapour was produced, which then condensed. Soot and carbon dioxide were also produced. When all the oxygen in the jar was used up, the candle went out.

Science activity

(!) Collect a small plastic dish, a candle and a wide-mouthed jam jar. Place the candle in the dish, and float the dish on water. Light the candle, and place the upturned jam jar over it. Watch what happens. Can you describe why it happens?

Your child will see the candle burn and then be extinguished. The dish holding the candle will rise up inside the jar as the oxygen is used up and water fills the space. The amount it rises can be used to estimate how much oxygen is in the air.

23 Is it hazardous?

Science facts
There are many substances that we handle, smell or eat. Not all substances are safe – some are hazardous. Some substances damage the skin, eyes or lungs; they are classified as irritant, harmful or corrosive, depending on the type of damage they do. Some substances harm us if they are eaten or breathed in; they are classified as toxic. Other substances are hazardous because they catch fire easily; they are classified as flammable. Always minimise the risks when dealing with any of these substances.

Science quiz
Draw a line joining each hazardous substance to the precautions you should take when dealing with it.

Hazardous substances	Precautions
Toxic solid	Avoid contact with skin and do not breathe in
Harmful spray	Do not spill on skin
Flammable spray	Do not eat or breathe in
Corrosive liquid	Keep away from fire

Science activity

(!) Look at some cleaning materials you can find in your home, such as bleach and furniture polish. What hazards and precautions are mentioned on their labels?

Encourage your child to examine the labels on products such as kitchen cleaners to find out if they are toxic, corrosive, flammable, etc. Take this opportunity to discuss the dangers of substances such as glues, acids and solvents with your child.

24 How does the water cycle work?

Science facts

Evaporation is the process by which water (a liquid) turns into water vapour (a gas). Condensation is the process by which water vapour turns back into water. Evaporation is quickened by heating, and condensation is quickened by cooling. Water from seas and rivers and from plants' leaves evaporates because of the Sun's heat. The water vapour gathers in the atmosphere. When this moisture-laden warm air meets colder air high in the atmosphere, it condenses to form clouds of tiny water droplets. When the droplets become big and heavy, they fall as rain. This rainwater soaks into the ground and eventually ends up back in rivers and seas.

Science quiz
Put a tick (✔) by the correct statements and a cross (✘) by the incorrect ones. Then decide whether or not statement 1 happens because of statement 2.

Statement 1	(✔) or (✘)	Statement 1 happens because of Statement 2 –True or False	Statement 2	(✔) or (✘)
Rain falls when clouds are formed.	✘	False	Water vapour condenses to form water when cooled.	✔
Water only evaporates from seas.	✘	False	Water vapour is formed faster when water is warmed.	✔
Water vapour condenses faster in the higher regions of the atmosphere.	✔	True	It is colder in the higher regions of the atmosphere.	✔

Science activity

Place an empty plastic bottle in a freezer for half an hour. Remove it, and pour a quarter of a teaspoon of water into the bottle. Screw on the cap, and leave it in a warm place for about an hour. What do you notice? Place the bottle back in the freezer for half an hour. What do you notice now?

In the activity, help your child to predict that the bottled water will disappear when put in a warm place and will return when the bottle cools. If this doesn't happen, repeat the activity using a smaller quantity of water and warmer conditions.

25 How does a condenser work?

Science facts
Water vapour will condense to form water when it cools. Condensers are devices that turn water vapour into water quickly. You can find condensers in many places, including power stations, laboratories and in air-conditioning systems. They work by allowing water vapour to meet a cold surface and condense back into liquid water. It is important to keep the surface cold. The surface normally gets heated by the vapour and so becomes less efficient. In a laboratory condenser, this warming up is prevented by placing the cold surface inside a jacket of cold, flowing water.

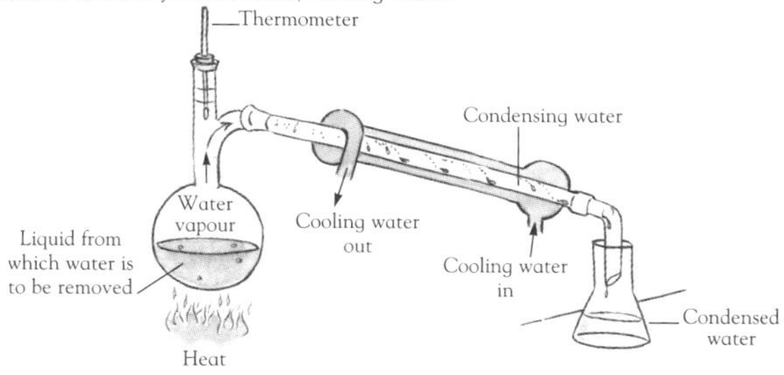

Science quiz
Sam looked at a kettle boiling. It produced steam that condensed on the window pane. After a while the condensation on the window disappeared. Explain why this happened.

As the steam heats up the pane, the condensed water evaporates.
The surface is no longer cold enough to condense water.

Science activity

(!) Ask an adult to help you with this experiment. Collect a sheet of card, a mirror and a plastic CD case. Use a steaming kettle to find out which is the best surface for condensing steam. Why do you think you got this result?

Take care when setting up the experiment: steam can cause severe burns. Boil a kettle so that the steam is directed towards the three surfaces. Try to make the comparison fair by placing the surfaces at the same distance from the kettle.

26 How soluble are materials?

Science facts
Substances that can be dissolved in a liquid are said to be soluble. Those that do not dissolve are said to be insoluble. The liquid in which a substance dissolves is called the solvent. The substance that is dissolved is called the solute. Together, they make a solution. Water is a good solvent: it dissolves many substances but not all. Sugar and salt both dissolve in water, while substances such as chalk and sand are insoluble.

Science quiz
Carol collected two different plant fertilisers from a garden centre. She was told to mix each fertiliser with water and then to sprinkle the solution on her plants. When she mixed them, the first substance "disappeared". The fertiliser in the second can sank to the bottom.

The fertiliser in the second watering can would not be very effective. Why?

It would not be effective because it is insoluble. It would not mix with the water and so would not be taken up by the plants' roots.

Science activity

Collect some substances such as flour, Epsom salts, icing sugar, sand, baking powder, bicarbonate of soda and cooking oil. Design a way of finding out which substances are soluble in water and which are insoluble.

Ask your child how he or she will know if a substance has dissolved. What will your child look for? Make sure that your child uses only small quantities of the solutes (baking powder, etc.) so that it is easy to see whether or not they dissolve.

27 Are all substances equally soluble?

Science facts
All soluble substances do not dissolve equally well. Sugar dissolves very easily, while other substances, such as salt, dissolve less easily. The amount of solute that will dissolve in a solvent is a measure of its solubility.

Science quiz
Below is a graph showing the solubility of different substances.

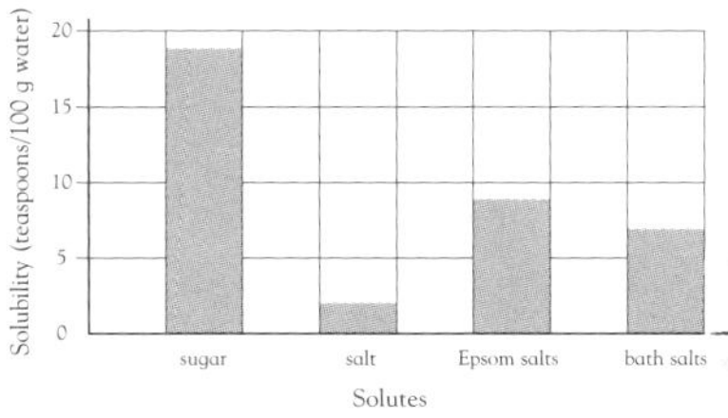

About how many spoonfuls of salt dissolve in the water? 2

About how many spoonfuls of bath salts dissolve in the water? 7

Another substance is more soluble than bath salts but less soluble than Epsom salts. What range of spoonfuls would you expect to dissolve? 7-9

List the solutes in the chart in order of their solubility.
Write the name of the most soluble substance first.

sugar   Epsom salts   bath salts   salt

Science activity

Does the grain size of sugar affect its solubility? Design and carry out an experiment to answer this question.

Ask your child to predict which size of sugar grain will dissolve more quickly in water and why. Help him or her plan an experiment. To make it fair, encourage your child to use the same amount of sugar and water in each instance.

28 Is water really pure?

Science facts
Tap water contains substances already dissolved in it. The amount and type of dissolved substance depends on where you live. This is why tap water tastes different in different areas. You can find out how much solute is dissolved in water by pouring a small amount into a glass and allowing it to evaporate. You will see a ring or some white scale left behind. Water that contains a lot of dissolved substances is called hard water, while water that contains very few dissolved substances is called soft water.

Science quiz
When Simon looked inside his kettle, he saw the inner wall was covered with a white scale, while inside his grandmother's kettle there was none. Can you explain why?

The white scale comes from solids dissolved in the water.
There are probably more solids dissolved in Simon's water.

Science activity

Pour some tap water into a saucer and allow it to evaporate. Look at the saucer to get an idea of what is dissolved in the water. Try the same experiment with some boiled water. Is there any difference?

The amount of solids dissolved in water depends on the area. Some areas have none. Others will have only a small amount. "Hard" water contains calcium and magnesium salts, which are the source of the "limescale" in household appliances.

29 Does temperature affect solubility?

Science facts
It is easier to dissolve soluble substances in warm water than in cold water. However, heat increases the solubility of some substances more than others.

Science quiz
Plot the following data on the graph. The data show the increase in solubility of table salt and of Epsom salts as temperature increases.

Temperature (°C)	Amount dissolved per jug (in grams)	
	Salt	Epsom salts
20	10	20
30	12	30
40	14	40
50	16	50
60	18	55

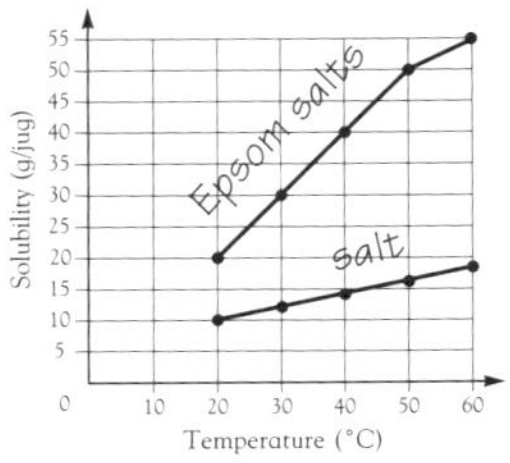

1 What pattern links the amount of table salt dissolved with temperature?
The hotter the water, the more salt it dissolves.

2 Is this pattern the same for Epsom salts?
The pattern is the same for Epsom salts.

3 What is different about the way temperature affects the solubility of table salt and Epsom salts?
The change in temperature affects the Epsom salts more.

(!) Find out how temperature affects the time taken for sugar to dissolve in water. Fill containers with equal quantities of water at different temperatures. You can do this by mixing different amounts of hot and cold water. Stir in equal amounts of sugar and compare the time taken for it to dissolve.

To make the test fair, use clear containers and add the same amount of water to each one. Use the same amount of sugar each time, and stir until it dissolves. Encourage your child to make a bar chart of his or her results.

30 Does adding salt change water?

Science facts
Mixing substances together can cause them to change. Adding salt to water makes the water taste salty. Objects float more easily in salt water than in fresh water. Salt water boils at a higher temperature than fresh water.

Science quiz
Look at the pairs of pictures. Which picture in each pair shows sea water and which shows fresh water?

fresh water

sea water

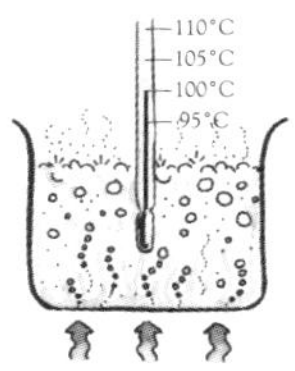

fresh water

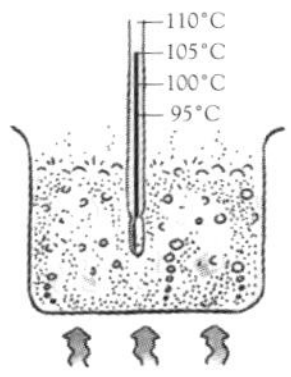

sea water

If you added sand to water, would it boil at a higher temperature?
No, because sand will not dissolve in water.

Science activity

Make a float from a cork and a screw (see diagram). Use the float in an experiment to investigate whether things float more easily as water gets more and more salty.

Your child will learn about the changes caused by mixing salt with water. Encourage your child to plan the experiment. He or she might start by adding one spoonful of salt, then two, and so on. The float will rise higher as the water gets saltier.

31 When do liquids freeze?

Science facts
Pure water freezes at 0°C. Water with substances dissolved in it (a solution) freezes at a lower temperature. Some substances, such as candle wax, freeze (solidify) at temperatures above 0°C. Other substances, such as vegetable oil, freeze at temperatures below 0°C. The temperature at which a substance freezes is called its freezing point.

Science quiz
The freezing points of different liquids are shown in the bar graph below.

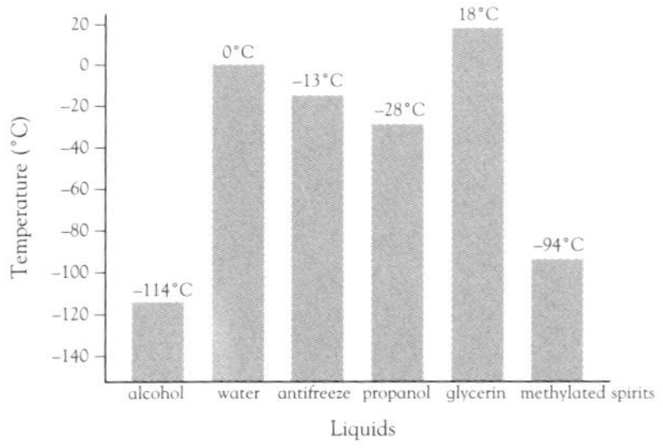

Looking at the bar graph, can you say which substance will be a solid on a winter's day but a liquid on a summer's day? The rhyme below will help you.

"5, 10 and 21 – winter, spring and summer sun."

Glycerin – it freezes at temperatures below 18°C.

Science activity

Try placing some oils in the freezer. You could use oils such as olive oil, walnut oil and vegetable oil. Which oil freezes first? What else do you notice about the effect of freezing on oils?

Your child will learn that different liquids have different freezing points. Only pure water freezes at 0°C. Encourage your child to notice that oils go cloudy as they reach their freezing points.

32 What do these words mean?

Draw a line joining each word to its definition.

Electrical conductor	Allows heat to pass through easily
Thermal conductor	Resistant to scratching
Thermal insulator	Allows electricity to pass through easily
Hard	Fixed volume, takes shape of container
Solid	Does not allow heat to pass through easily
Liquid	Fills all the available space and flows easily
Gas	Allows water to soak through
Permeable	Retains its shape and does not flow
Condense	To change from a liquid to a solid
Evaporate	To mix a solute in a solvent
Solvent	To change from a liquid to a gas
Solidify (freeze)	To change from a gas to a liquid
Melt	A substance that does not dissolve easily
Dissolve	A substance that dissolves easily
Solute	A substance that dissolves other substances
Soluble	A mixture of a solute and a solvent
Insoluble	To change from a solid to a liquid
Solution	A substance that dissolves in a solvent

This page marks your child's successful completion of this book. Encourage your child to refer back to earlier pages in the book to work out the answers and so create a glossary. Congratulate your child on finishing the book.

How fast do things cool down?

Science facts

Hot water cools down until it reaches room temperature. There is a pattern in the way things cool down.

Science quiz

Look at the axes on the graph below. Guess the shape of a line showing how hot water cools down. Draw this line on the graph. Julia did an experiment to see what really happens. Her results are shown in the table on the right. Plot her results on your graph. Does it match the drawing you made earlier?

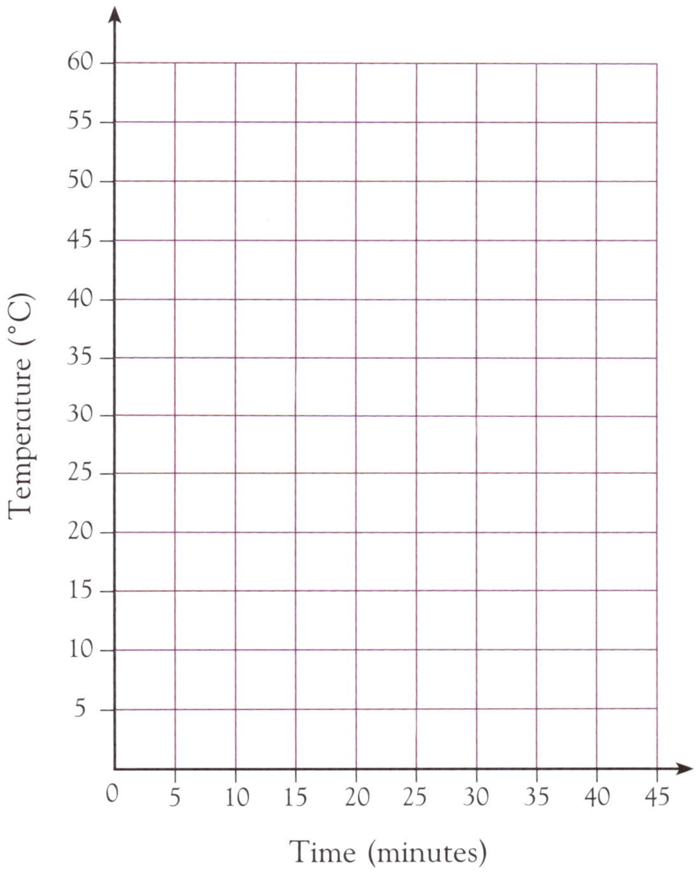

Cooling time	Temperature of water
0 minutes	60°C
5 minutes	40°C
10 minutes	28°C
15 minutes	24°C
20 minutes	23°C
25 minutes	22°C
30 minutes	22°C
35 minutes	22°C

What will the temperature be after 45 minutes? ....

Science activity

(!) Measure the temperature of some hot water as it cools down. Take the temperature every 3 minutes. Plot a graph of your results. What shape is your graph? Is your graph similar to the one you plotted above?

How quickly does it evaporate?

Science facts

Water left in a bowl will slowly disappear. It turns into water vapour, and mixes with the air. This means the water has evaporated: the liquid has changed into a gas. Some liquids evaporate more quickly than others. Liquids with high boiling points (those that boil at very high temperatures) tend to evaporate more slowly than those with lower boiling points.

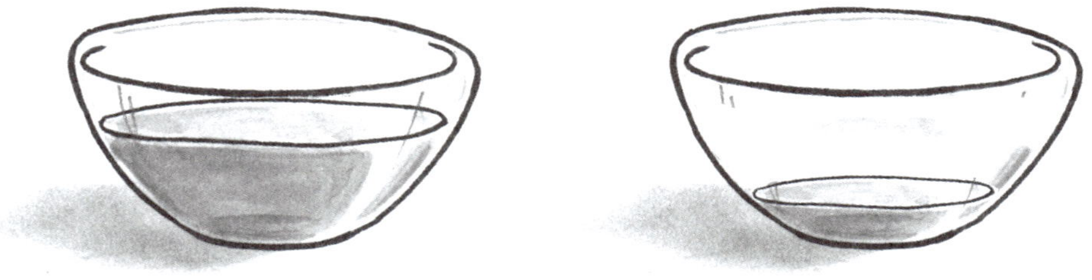

Science quiz

Number the three liquids listed below in order of how fast you would expect them to evaporate. Explain why you think so.

☐ nail-polish remover ☐ water ☐ butane propellant from an aerosol spray

....

....

....

How do you think you could make the water evaporate more quickly?

....

....

Science activity

Drops of water on your skin evaporate quickly because of the warmth of your body. As the water evaporates, it takes heat from your skin. Smear a few drops of water over the palm of one hand. Do they disappear? Does your palm feel hot or cold?

Can you separate salt from sand?

Science facts

Filtering removes insoluble particles from water (particles that do not dissolve). Salt is soluble in water, but sand is not soluble (it is insoluble). The water in a salt solution will evaporate if it is left uncovered. Rock salt is a mixture of salt and sand.

Science quiz

Using the information above, explain how you could separate the salt from a piece of rock salt. Drawing a flow chart might help.

Science activity

What type of paper makes the best filter? Design an experiment to find out. You will need a funnel and different kinds of paper – newspaper, writing paper, blotting paper, wrapping paper and tissue paper.

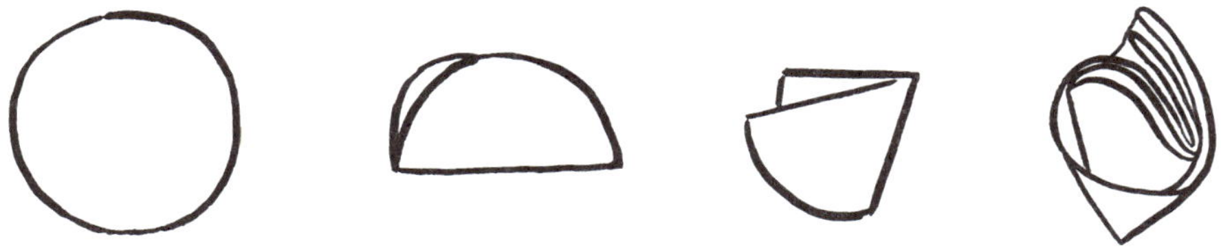

Are some changes reversible?

Science facts

When ice is warmed, it melts to form water. When water is heated further, it boils to form water vapour. These changes from solid to liquid to gas can be reversed by cooling water vapour. The water vapour will condense to form water, and the water will freeze to form ice.

Ice — melts → Water — boils → Water vapour

Water vapour — condenses → Water — freezes → Ice

Science quiz

Explain what is happening to the water in each picture.

....

....

....

....

....

....

Science activity

(!) Light a candle, and watch it carefully (do not touch it or get too close). Can you identify the solid wax, melted wax and wax vapour? Can you see the liquid wax solidifying when the flame is put out?

Are some changes irreversible?

Science facts

When you mix substances together, they may change to form new substances. The changes can be reversible or irreversible. For instance, when vinegar is mixed with bicarbonate of soda, the two fizz and a new substance is formed. This change is irreversible. A change is likely to be irreversible if there is a reaction, such as a fizz or a temperature change.

Science quiz

Are the following mixing processes reversible or irreversible?

1 Stirring sugar into water ....

2 Adding water to plaster of Paris ....

3 Mixing sand and sugar ....

4 Adding lemon juice to red-cabbage juice (the colour changes from purple to red) ....

Science activity

Try mixing the following substances. Which changes are reversible?

1 Lemon juice added to baking powder
2 Vinegar added to chalk
3 Vinegar added to salt
4 Lemon juice added to sugar

What happens when it burns?

Science facts

Oxygen from the air is needed for something to burn. Burning is an irreversible process that forms new substances. Some of these substances are solids, such as ash or soot, and some are gases, such as water vapour and carbon dioxide. When paper burns, it produces soot, water vapour, carbon dioxide, a small amount of other gases and ash.

Science quiz

Look at the drawing. It shows a candle burning inside an upturned jam jar.

What do you think is produced when the wax burns? Explain why you think this.

....

....

....

Science activity

(!) Collect a small plastic dish, a candle and a wide-mouthed jam jar. Place the candle in the dish, and float the dish on water. Light the candle, and place the upturned jam jar over it. Watch what happens. Can you describe why it happens?

Is it hazardous?

Science facts

There are many substances that we handle, smell or eat. Not all substances are safe – some are hazardous. Some substances damage the skin, eyes or lungs; they are classified as irritant, harmful or corrosive, depending on the type of damage they do. Some substances harm us if they are eaten or breathed in; they are classified as toxic. Other substances are hazardous because they catch fire easily; they are classified as flammable. Always minimise the risks when dealing with any of these substances.

Science quiz

Draw a line joining each hazardous substance to the precautions you should take when dealing with it.

Hazardous substances	Precautions
Toxic solid	Avoid contact with skin and do not breathe in
Harmful spray	Do not spill on skin
Flammable spray	Do not eat or breathe in
Corrosive liquid	Keep away from fire

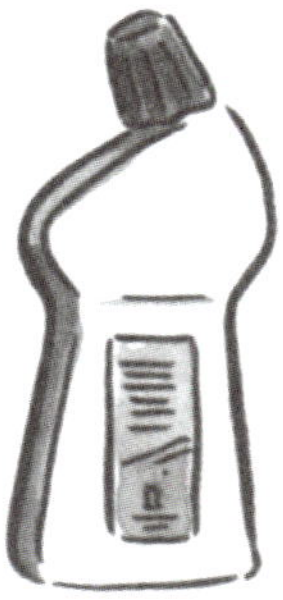

Science activity

(!) Look at some cleaning materials you can find in your home, such as bleach and furniture polish. What hazards and precautions are mentioned on their labels?

How does the water cycle work?

Science facts

Evaporation is the process by which water (a liquid) turns into water vapour (a gas). Condensation is the process by which water vapour turns back into water. Evaporation is quickened by heating, and condensation is quickened by cooling. Water from seas and rivers and from plants' leaves evaporates because of the Sun's heat. The water vapour gathers in the atmosphere. When this moisture-laden warm air meets colder air high in the atmosphere, it condenses to form clouds of tiny water droplets. When the droplets become big and heavy, they fall as rain. This rainwater soaks into the ground and eventually ends up back in rivers and seas.

Science quiz

Put a tick (✔) by the correct statements and a cross (✘) by the incorrect ones. Then decide whether or not statement 1 happens because of statement 2.

Statement 1	(✔) or (✘)	Statement 1 happens because of Statement 2 –True or False	Statement 2	(✔) or (✘)
Rain falls when clouds are formed.			Water vapour condenses to form water when cooled.	
Water only evaporates from seas.			Water vapour is formed faster when water is warmed.	
Water vapour condenses faster in the higher regions of the atmosphere.			It is colder in the higher regions of the atmosphere.	

Science activity

Place a large, empty plastic bottle in a freezer for half an hour. Remove it, and pour a quarter of a teaspoon of water into the bottle. Screw on the cap, and leave it in a warm place for an hour. What do you notice? Place the bottle back in the freezer for half an hour. What do you notice now?

How does a condenser work?

Science facts

Water vapour will condense to form water when it cools. Condensers are devices that turn water vapour into water quickly. You can find condensers in many places, including power stations, laboratories and in air-conditioning systems. They work by allowing water vapour to meet a cold surface and condense back into liquid water. It is important to keep the surface cold. The surface normally gets heated by the vapour and so becomes less efficient. In a laboratory condenser, this warming up is prevented by placing the cold surface inside a jacket of cold, flowing water.

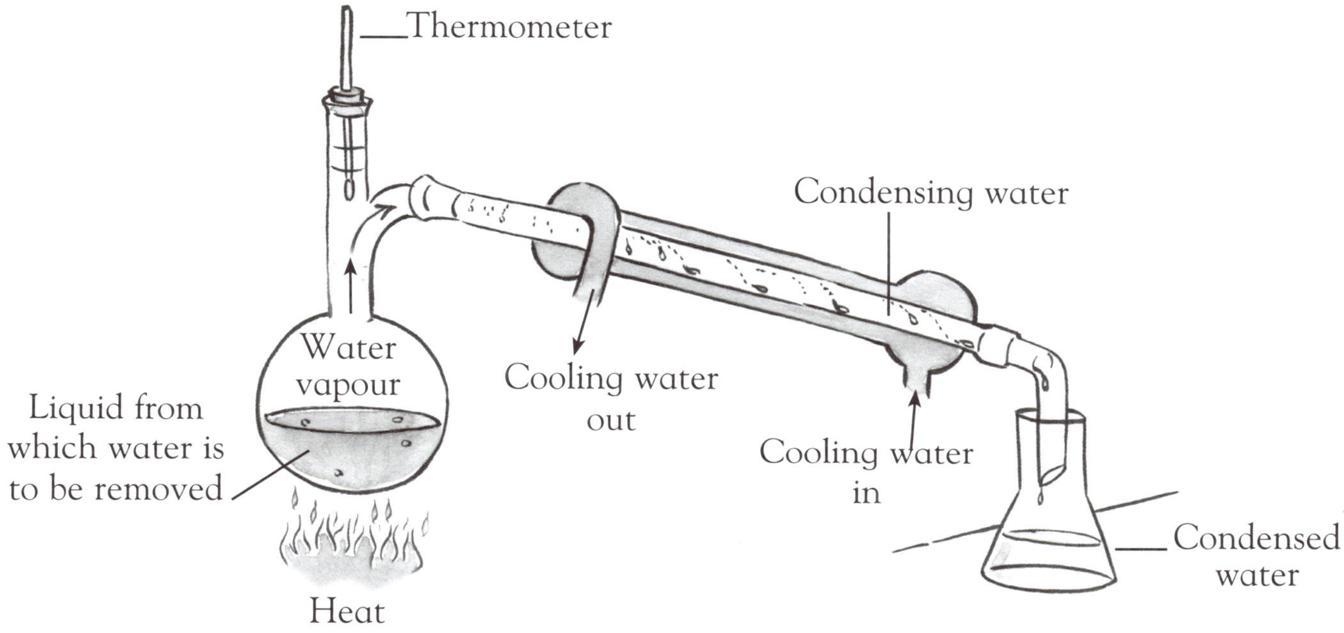

Science quiz

Sam looked at a kettle boiling. It produced steam that condensed on the window pane. After a while the condensation on the window disappeared. Explain why this happened.

....

....

Science activity

(!) Ask an adult to help you with this experiment. Collect a sheet of card, a mirror and a plastic CD case. Use a steaming kettle to find out which is the best surface for condensing steam. Why do you think you got this result?

How soluble are materials?

Science facts

Substances that can be dissolved in a liquid are said to be soluble. Those that do not dissolve are said to be insoluble. The liquid in which a substance dissolves is called the solvent. The substance that is dissolved is called the solute. Together, they make a solution. Water is a good solvent: it dissolves many substances but not all. Sugar and salt both dissolve in water, while substances such as chalk and sand are insoluble.

Science quiz

Carol collected two different plant fertilisers from a garden centre. She was told to mix each fertiliser with water and then to sprinkle the solution on her plants. When she mixed them, the first substance "disappeared". The fertiliser in the second can sank to the bottom.

The fertiliser in the second watering can would not be very effective. Why?

....

....

Science activity

Collect some substances such as flour, Epsom salts, icing sugar, sand, baking powder, bicarbonate of soda and cooking oil. Design a way of finding out which substances are soluble in water and which are insoluble.

Are all substances equally soluble?

Science facts

All soluble substances do not dissolve equally well. Sugar dissolves very easily, while other substances, such as salt, dissolve less easily. The amount of solute that will dissolve in a solvent is a measure of its solubility.

Science quiz

Below is a graph showing the solubility of different substances.

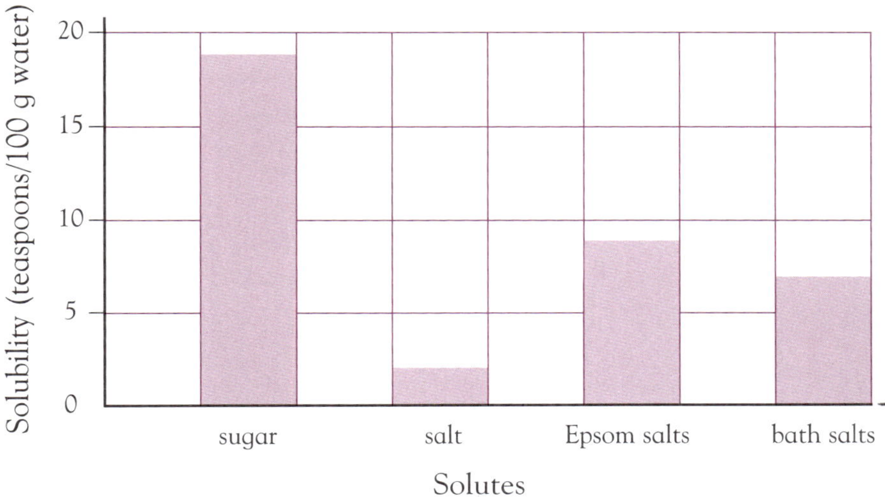

About how many spoonfuls of salt dissolve in the water?

About how many spoonfuls of bath salts dissolve in the water?

Another substance is more soluble than bath salts but less soluble than Epsom salts. What range of spoonfuls would you expect to dissolve?

List the solutes in the chart in order of their solubility.
Write the name of the most soluble substance first.

....

Science activity

Does the grain size of sugar affect its solubility? Design and carry out an experiment to answer this question.

Is water really pure?

Science facts

Tap water contains substances already dissolved in it. The amount and type of dissolved substance depends on where you live. This is why tap water tastes different in different areas. You can find out how much solute is dissolved in water by pouring a small amount into a glass and allowing it to evaporate. You will see a ring or some white scale left behind. Water that contains a lot of dissolved substances is called hard water, while water that contains very few dissolved substances is called soft water.

Science quiz

When Simon looked inside his kettle, he saw the inner wall was covered with a white scale, while inside his grandmother's kettle there was none. Can you explain why?

....

....

Science activity

Pour some tap water into a saucer and allow it to evaporate. Look at the saucer to get an idea of what is dissolved in the water. Try the same experiment with some boiled water. Is there any difference?

Does temperature affect solubility?

Science facts

It is easier to dissolve soluble substances in warm water than in cold water. However, heat increases the solubility of some substances more than others.

Science quiz

Plot the following data on the graph. The data show the increase in solubility of table salt and of Epsom salts as temperature increases.

Temperature (°C)	Amount dissolved per jug (in grams)	
	Salt	Epsom salts
20	10	20
30	12	30
40	14	40
50	16	50
60	18	55

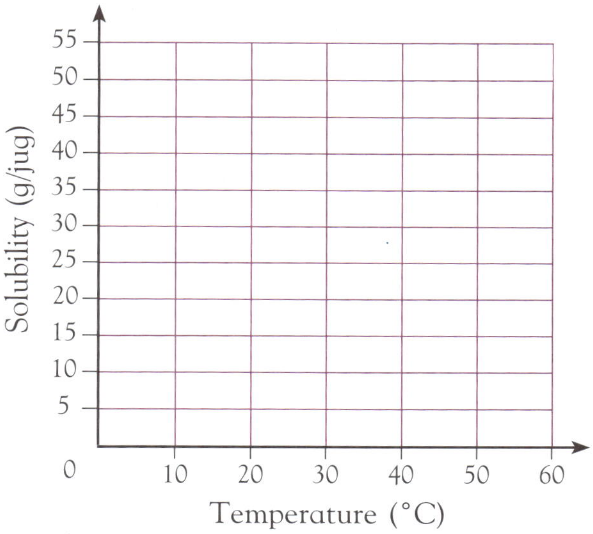

1 What pattern links the amount of table salt dissolved with temperature?

....

2 Is this pattern the same for Epsom salts?

....

3 What is different about the way temperature affects the solubility of table salt and Epsom salts?

....

Science activity

(!) Find out how temperature affects the time taken for sugar to dissolve in water. Fill containers with equal quantities of water at different temperatures. You can do this by mixing different amounts of hot and cold water. Stir in equal amounts of sugar and compare the time taken for it to dissolve.

Does adding salt change water?

Science facts

Mixing substances together can cause them to change. Adding salt to water makes the water taste salty. Objects float more easily in salt water than in fresh water. Salt water boils at a higher temperature than fresh water.

Science quiz

Look at the pairs of pictures. Which picture in each pair shows sea water and which shows fresh water?

....

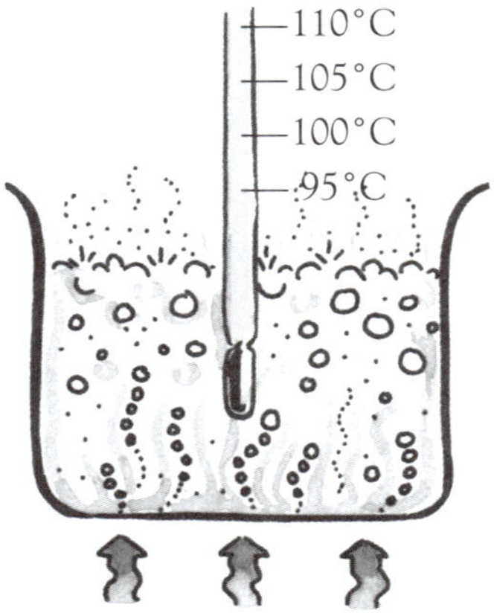

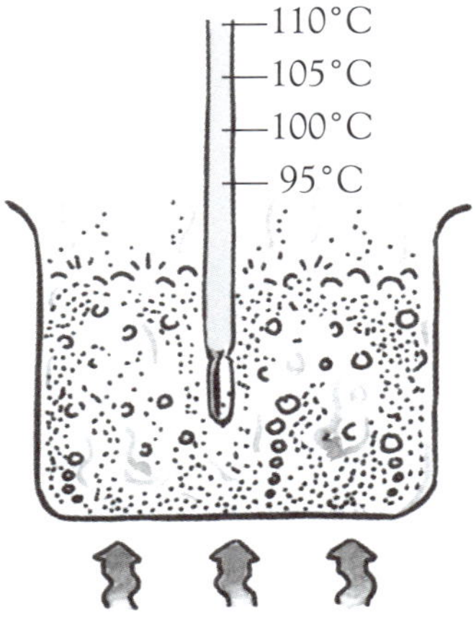

....

If you added sand to water, would it boil at a higher temperature?

....

Science activity

Make a float from a cork and a screw (see diagram). Use the float in an experiment to investigate whether things float more easily as water gets more and more salty.

When do liquids freeze?

Science facts

Pure water freezes at 0°C. Water with substances dissolved in it (a solution) freezes at a lower temperature. Some substances, such as candle wax, freeze (solidify) at temperatures above 0°C. Other substances, such as vegetable oil, freeze at temperatures below 0°C. The temperature at which a substance freezes is called its freezing point.

Science quiz

The freezing points of different liquids are shown in the bar graph below.

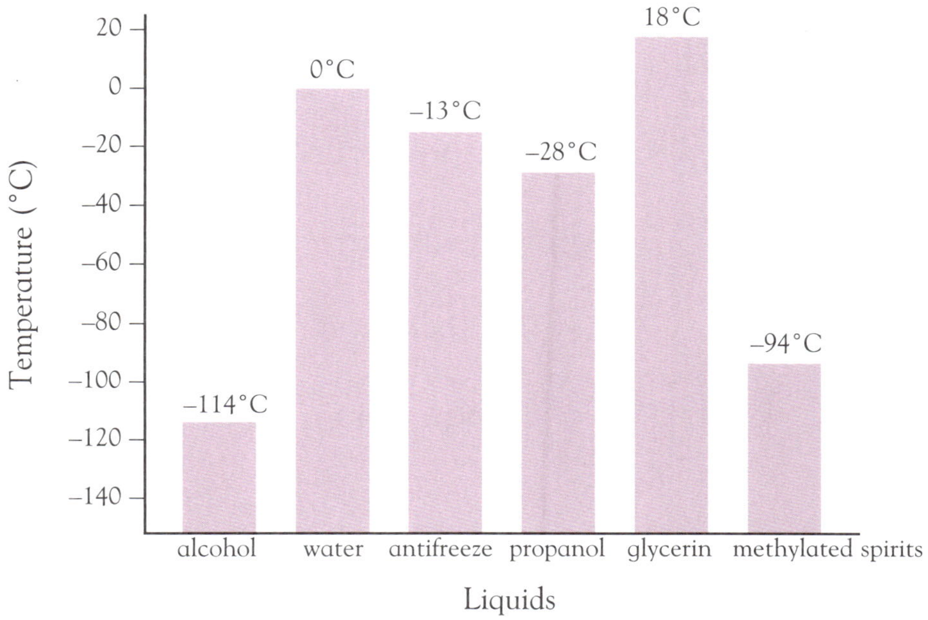

Looking at the bar graph, can you say which substance will be a solid on a winter's day but a liquid on a summer's day? The rhyme below will help you.

"5, 10 and 21 – winter, spring and summer sun."

Science activity

Try placing some oils in the freezer. You could use oils such as olive oil, walnut oil and vegetable oil. Which oil freezes first? What else do you notice about the effect of freezing on oils?

What do these words mean?

Draw a line joining each word to its definition.

Electrical conductor	Allows heat to pass through easily
Thermal conductor	Resistant to scratching
Thermal insulator	Allows electricity to pass through easily
Hard	Fixed volume, takes shape of container
Solid	Does not allow heat to pass through easily
Liquid	Fills all the available space and flows easily
Gas	Allows water to soak through
Permeable	Retains its shape and does not flow
Condense	To change from a liquid to a solid
Evaporate	To mix a solute in a solvent
Solvent	To change from a liquid to a gas
Solidify (freeze)	To change from a gas to a liquid
Melt	A substance that does not dissolve easily
Dissolve	A substance that dissolves easily
Solute	A substance that dissolves other substances
Soluble	A mixture of a solute and a solvent
Insoluble	To change from a solid to a liquid
Solution	A substance that dissolves in a solvent